An African Education

An African Education

FROM VILLAGE SCHOOL TO CAP AND GOWN
A HISTORY OF THE SALIKENNI SCHOLARSHIP FUND

DONALD H. MAY

White River Press • Amherst, Massachusetts

An African Education

First published 2014.

White River Press
PO Box 3561
Amherst, MA 01004
www.whiteriverpress.com

www.salikenni.org

Book and cover design and map illustration:
Douglas Lufkin
Lufkin Graphic Designs
www.LufkinGraphics.com

ISBN: 978-1-887043-12-0

Photographs by the author, SSF volunteers and students.

Library of Congress Cataloging-in-Publication Data

May, Donald H.
An African education : stories of challenge and triumph in establishing the Salikenni Scholarship Fund in the Gambia / by Donald H. May.
    pages cm
    ISBN 978-1-887043-12-0 (pbk. : alk. paper)
1. Salikenni Scholarship Fund. 2. Scholarships--Gambia. 3. Poor children--Education--Gambia. I. Title.
LB2849.G3M39 2014
371.2'23096651--dc23
                        2014015773

To the SSF students,
past, present and future.

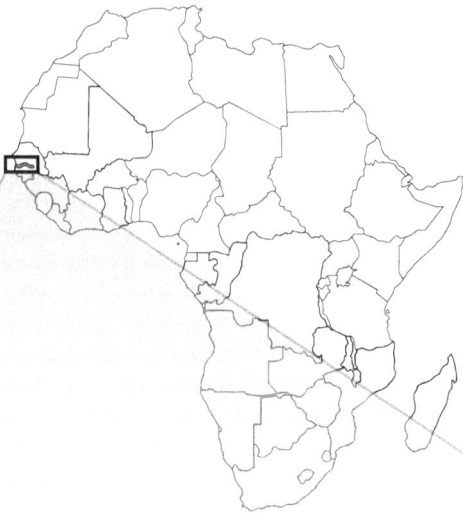

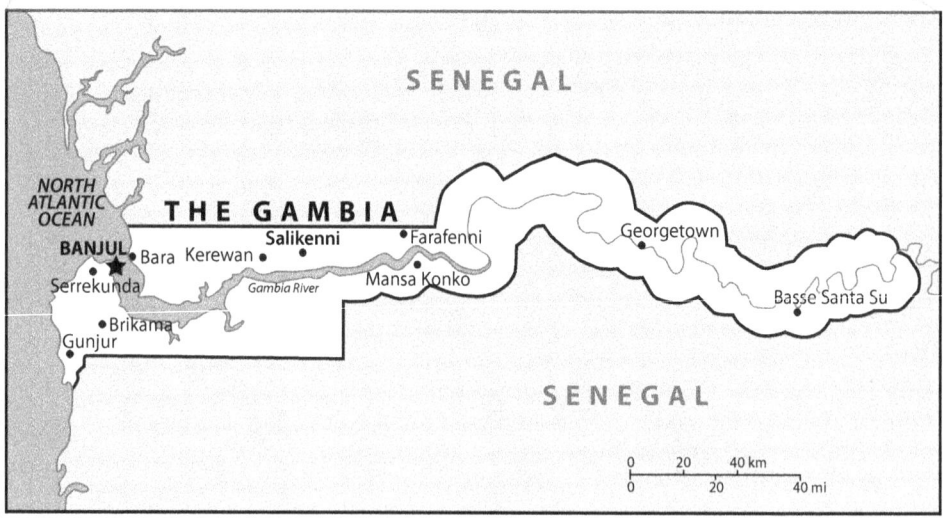

Contents

Preface

IT BEGAN WITH AN EARLY MORNING WALK through the village. The rising sun, red and huge, cast a pink glow on the whitewashed walls and corrugated metal roofs. A tall girl approached on the sandy lane and walked beside me for a few minutes in silence. Then she asked in a shy voice: "Can you pay my school fees?"

That was the origin of a scholarship program that my wife, Alison, and I started in 1996 in the village of Salikenni in a rural part of The Gambia in West Africa.

When I asked people in the village about the girl, they said that many children were dropping out of school because their parents could not afford the fees charged by the government school system. In sub-Saharan Africa today most countries still cannot afford to provide free public education for all their children.

We formed a nonprofit organization in the United States called the Salikenni Scholarship Fund (SSF). We raised money through individual contributions, and we began awarding scholarships. Every year since then we have selected, from Salikenni and several nearby villages, a few of the neediest boys and girls who we believe also have academic ability. We usually start sponsoring them when they reach grade seven. We tell them that, if they can make it, we will pay for their education through middle school, high school, and four years at the University of The Gambia.

This account describes the evolution of one small program in one tiny corner of Africa, our mistakes, our setbacks and our successes. It provides a view at the local level of education problems that are widespread in Africa, including access to and quality of education, the importance of reading skills, challenges involved in educating girls, and the scarcity of well-paying jobs at the end of school.

But this book is really about our students. They are an extraordinary group. They come from very poor families; their parents, for the most part, have never been to school. It is rare to find books in their homes. To get an education these students must overcome huge obstacles. They struggle to learn a confusing language, English, often from teachers who have barely mastered it themselves. They attend overcrowded classes where sometimes there are no textbooks. To go to high school they must move to the metropolitan area of the country and live with relatives, sometimes in crowded conditions that make it very difficult to study.

All are motivated by the belief that, through education, they will be able to pull themselves and their families out of poverty. Some have failed, but many have succeeded and are now in or have graduated from the university.

Gradually our students have become a closely knit group and often speak of themselves as "a family." The senior students tutor and mentor the younger ones. Grade ten students who are good at one subject help other tenth graders who are struggling with that subject.

In 2012 a group of our university-level students, with our strong agreement, formed a local management board and now manage the SSF program in The Gambia. They are determined to keep it going for younger generations far into the future. Alison and I, and our contributors, will continue to help them by raising funds.

Their education has also been our education. Their individual stories show what the human spirit can accomplish under adversity.

Don May

August 2014

Acknowledgments

THIS BOOK COULD NOT HAVE BEEN WRITTEN without the assistance and work of many people. The Salikenni Scholarship Fund could not have taken shape or survived without the support of an incredibly loyal group of donors who have stuck with us year after year. Our financing comes from individuals and is generally in small amounts.

I owe profound thanks to my wife, Alison. Without her practical common sense the program would have gone astray many times. Without her patient record-keeping we would not have been able to keep track of our students. She traveled with me to The Gambia in June 2007 and has worked tirelessly over the years as co-administrator of SSF.

Thanks are also due to others who journeyed with me to Salikenni and provided the program with both hard work and wise advice:

- Rob Edson, then principal of the Marion Cross School in Norwich, Vermont, who came with me in February 2007.
- Anne S. Segal, of Hanover, New Hampshire, a retired teacher and school administrator and former Peace Corps volunteer in Namibia, Africa, who joined me for a week in November 2007. Anne closely observed the program and continues to offer wise advice.

- Robert Scobie, also of Hanover, a retired special education teacher, came with me in March 2008. Bob gave the village school a set of phonics teaching materials, which he had prepared himself, and coached Salikenni teachers in their use. He also continues to provide valuable advice.
- Our son, David, accompanied me in 2009 and provided more insights and advice.
- Mary Ann Roberts, a financial planner, and her husband, Bill Babcock, a lawyer, both of Alexandria, Virginia, came with me to the village in October 2011, and immediately bonded with our students. They distributed red book bags, pencils and pens, bought at their own expense, and engaged the students in games with flashcards. They also arranged, at their own expense, for repairs to the hand pump that waters the school garden. In November 2012 Mary Ann and Bill returned to The Gambia and Salikenni and brought more supplies for individual students. They participated in the second of the two meetings at which our senior students took charge of the management of the program.

Every writer needs a good editor. I am lucky to have three good ones: initially Alison, then our daughter, Libby May, and finally Jean Stone, who along with others on the White River Press team, Linda L. Roghaar and Douglas J. Lufkin, had sufficient faith in the book to get it into print.

Most of all, my thanks go to our students in The Gambia. To the extent that we have succeeded at all, that success is fundamentally theirs.

DHM

An African Education

CHAPTER 1

"We Will Succeed"

OUSMAN JARJU remembers clearly the day he was told he would be the first in his immediate family to go to school.

He was nine years old, two years beyond the normal age for starting grade one at the government school in the village of Salikenni. His older brother and three older sisters had received no schooling except for classes in Islam and the Koran; their father, Yahya Jarju, had the same plan for Ousman. Every working day during the growing season, Yahya took young Ousman to the fields outside the village. At first Ousman sat in the shade while his father worked. Soon he was walking beside the two huge bulls that pulled the plow, guiding them in a straight line, while his father walked behind, holding the wooden handles of the plow. This went on year after year.

But a benevolent man named Njundu Fadera had his eye on Ousman. Fadera was a teacher, a citizen of the village and a distant relative. (Years later he became the principal of the village school.)

"One day," Ousman recalled, "Fadera said to me, 'Tomorrow I'm coming for you. You're going to school.' It was Fadera who put me in school. He persuaded my father."

Ousman Jarju.

Salikenni is a village of about 3,500 people in the rural North Bank region of The Gambia, a small country in West Africa. The village is a network of sand lanes that jog and curve like the streets of a medieval European town. On both sides of the lanes are family compounds, most of which are enclosed in some fashion for privacy. Some are surrounded by substantial walls of cement block, painted or whitewashed. Others have fences made of scraps of rusty corrugated metal, often with jagged edges, nailed to crooked wooden poles. A few fences are woven from reeds.

The village sits on a wide, slightly rolling plain of grasslands and scattered trees, just out of sight of the broad Gambia River. It's a compact village. Almost everyone is a farmer. But no one lives among the farms; everyone lives within the village. People go to the countryside each day to tend their fields, then they return by nightfall.

As we approach Salikenni (just around the bend) a greeting party appears. The first in a stately row of lush mango trees is visible on the left.

Because the village is situated on a narrow sand road that loops away from the region's paved highway, there is little motorized traffic. A few cars, trucks and dilapidated passenger vans pass by slowly; horse and donkey carts are much more common. Young boys ride, bareback, atop horses and donkeys, steering them through the village, then lining them up at watering places for a drink.

A group of women welcome us on a Salikenni lane. The jagged, metal fence in the background provides privacy for a family compound.

During much of the year, goats and sheep freely wander the streets. But during the farming season, owners must keep them tied up, and there is a fine if they are found nibbling crops. Gambian sheep have very short hair. As a village man once explained to me, "Would you wear a wool coat here?"

The government school is a cluster of whitewashed buildings at the edge of the village. There are one or two much smaller Arabic schools, or *dara*, where the Arabic language and the Koran are taught. There is a big mosque with tall minarets and several smaller mosques. There is a covered market place and a government health center. A youth center, built by private donors from Germany, houses a nursery school. Several small shops sell locally baked bread, tinned food, cooking oil by the cup, sugar in little plastic bags, flashlight batteries, candles and single cigarettes. It is common to see young men smoking in the streets. Low platforms called *banteba*, made of wooden poles or bamboo and designed for sitting or reclining, are located at several intersections throughout the village. Old men congregate there, talking politics and surveying the scene.

The village is a mixture of old and new. A rural electrification project reached this area in 2007—a row of tall, cast-concrete poles now runs down the main sand street and along some side streets. Many households now have electric lights, for which they buy prepaid credit from an office in the village. When the credit is exhausted, their lights blink off without warning. Almost everyone has a mobile phone. Cell phone technology has largely leapfrogged landlines, which are expensive to install. Visitors are sometimes surprised to see a boy driving a donkey cart with the reins in one hand and a cell phone in the other, pressed against his ear.

Salikenni has one huge asset that villages in many parts of Africa still lack: clean water. The World Bank and other international donors have installed solar-powered pumping systems in many villages throughout The Gambia. Water is pumped from a secure, enclosed well on relatively high ground outside Salikenni. It goes up into a large tank that stands on stilts, then flows through underground pipes to public taps at different locations in the village. Women and girls do the family's laundry in plastic basins at the public taps. They also fill buckets, basins, or yellow plastic

Another village lane. Baobab trees (in the background) are as fat as and the same color as elephants.

"jerry" cans with clean water and carry them on their heads back to their compounds for drinking and bathing. I have often marveled at the physical strength and skill of these women and girls. With just a little help from one of her companions to raise the heavy basin onto her head, each woman then walks, straight-backed, to her compound. To make it through the doorway into her house, she must stoop slightly while pushing back a curtain with one hand and steadying the basin on her head with the other. This is done in one continuous motion as she crosses the threshold and steps out of her plastic flip-flops, leaving them neatly on the ground outside the door. She seldom spills a drop. Some visitors purify this water, but I have always drunk it straight, with no ill effects.

The majority of people living in Salikenni are of the Mandinka tribe. The ethnic groups in The Gambia are Mandinka (42 percent), Fula (18 percent), Wolof (16 percent), and a number of smaller groups. These tribes coexist with virtually no violence and only a modest amount of political rivalry. Each group has its own language.

The Mandinka language is full of elaborate greetings. When two people pass in the street, one says *Suumoolee* (su-MOH-lay), which literally means "Where are your people?," but to them it asks "How are your people?"

The second person responds *I be jee* (ee-bay-JAY), "They are there," meaning "They are fine."

I la musolee (ee la mu-SO-lay), says the first person, "Where (how) is your wife?" Or, *I la kemo*, (ee la KAYmo), "Where is your husband?"

A be jee (ah bay JAY), "She or he is there."

Kortanante, "I hope there is no trouble."

Tanante, "No trouble."

Alhamdulillah!, "Praise God."

The first person may continue, asking about brothers, sisters, cousins and aunts. Then the flow reverses like a rapid tide, and the second person asks the same questions back.

People in the urban area of The Gambia often don't take the time for this ritual, but rural people consider it an art form. A visitor can have quite a long and friendly conversation with a village resident by only learning these simple greetings.

Rural Gambians are above all a conversational people. They cluster in small groups along the village lanes, talking in animated tones. Come evening, large families—grandmothers, parents, aunts, uncles and small children—sit in the courtyards of their compounds and talk long into the night. People stroll from compound to compound exchanging greetings and news.

Almost everyone in Salikenni is a Muslim. There is no Christian church in the village. The Gambia is 90 percent Muslim and 9 percent Christian. In the village Islam is on the surface of everyday life. The muezzins in the mosques issue their slow, lilting calls to prayer over loudspeakers. Many Salikenni people, men and women, pray five times a day. People walk around fingering prayer beads.

People leaving Salikenni's main mosque after Friday prayers.

The religion is imbedded in daily language, with many words and phrases imported from Arabic: "I will come to your compound this evening, *Inshallah*," which means "God willing." Just before entering a neighbor's compound, a person will say *Salaam Alekum* (peace be upon you) and someone inside will respond *Malekum Salaam* (and you). I have never heard a Salikenni Muslim advocate violence. The residents shake their heads sadly over news of suicide bombings or other killings elsewhere in the world. They say the Prophet Mohammed taught that killing is wrong. One very old man in the village once told me that the reason we are different colors is that "Allah used clay of different colors when he made us."

The sounds of the village are as distinctive as the sights. Walking along its lanes at almost any time of day, you can hear from behind a compound wall the rhythmic thump-thump of a woman or girl pounding grain. This is always the work of females. They put the grain into a wooden mortar that is nearly three feet tall, then they pound it with a wooden pestle the size of an American baseball bat until the grain is a fine powder. Often two girls pound together in the same mortar, alternating their strokes, resulting in a double thump-thump, thump-thump. Sometimes three girls make a game of pounding together, and it sounds like a galloping horse. But this usually ends in giggles when one girl breaks the rhythm.

Women and girls pound rice and other grains in large wooden mortars, with pestles the size of baseball bats. Here two are pounding with alternating strokes.

Another typical sound is the soft who-who-WHO of the *pura*, the local name of a kind of dove. Whenever I hear it, I think, "Now I am in The Gambia."

Sometimes these village sounds merge into a symphony. On one of my early visits, I stayed in a room near the center of the village. Every morning I awoke to the same sequence of sounds. First a rooster crowed when it was still pitch dark. Then a donkey in his nearby pen brayed in a loud series of gasps that sounded like a rusty engine trying to start. Then the muezzin in the nearest mosque began his call to prayer. He was soon joined by another muezzin a little farther away. Their calls echoed through the village almost in counterpoint so it was hard to tell if there were two callers or many more. Then suddenly there was complete silence, and I knew that people were in the mosques at prayer. It was still very dark.

The sun rises as an enormous red ball in Salikenni. During the day the length of a person's shadow indicates the times for prayer. The heat from the midday sun is like a physical blow to the body. The Gambia is 13 degrees above the equator. Shade is precious. People gather in shady areas of their compounds—under an orange tree or next to a wall—to sit and talk or to work at tasks such as sorting groundnuts (peanuts) or mending fishing nets. As the sun's angle changes they have to keep moving their chairs and mats from one spot to another. The sun heats the metal roofs and turns the houses into ovens. It takes a long time in the evening for the interiors to cool down. That is why Gambians stay up very late at night, chatting in the courtyards of their compounds.

———◆◆◆◆———

Ousman Jarju's family compound is typical of many in the village. It's a cluster of buildings with fading whitewashed walls and rusting corrugated metal roofs, arranged around a courtyard of brown sand. The fence in front is made from old corrugated metal roofing. The front gate is not hinged but is simply a lattice of sticks that is lifted into place at night and moved to one side in the morning.

The Jarju compound in Salikenni is always full of kids, and they all show up when a camera appears.

On a recent early morning visit I found the compound bustling with activity. Three girls were taking turns pounding grain. Several women were leaving for their rice fields with basins on their heads. A donkey hitched to a cart waited patiently for a trip to a nearby village. There were enough small children running about to populate a nursery school.

Ousman's father, Yahya, is a hearty man of sixty. He has a broad smile, which causes his dark face to become a field of wrinkles. He wears traditional African clothes: a loose-fitting, knee-length robe over cotton trousers and a round cap on his head. He has been a farmer all his life. He says he was "born farming." When he was young he learned the Arabic alphabet from a scholar in the village. At every prayer time during the day he reads a passage from the Koran in Arabic. But he has never been to the government school and does not speak or read English.

Ousman's mother, Binta Kinteh, is a thin woman with kind and thoughtful eyes. She has never been to school either.

Yahya explained to me (with Ousman translating) that years ago he had had mixed feelings about education. He believed—as his own father did—that the role of children was to provide labor on the farm. Yet he had begun to notice that some families sent their children to school and that some of these children grew up and got jobs and now were supporting the folks at home.

Yahya also observed that farming alone "does not sustain the family." During his lifetime, farming in the Salikenni area has not changed one bit, he said. It was still "the same methods, the same crops, the same yield." Almost every Salikenni family, in order to survive, depends on some member of the extended family who has moved to the urban area or to the United States or Europe and sends small amounts of money home. But Yahya's family had no such benefactor. So when Njundu Fadera urged him to send Ousman to school, Yahya agreed.

Pounding grain is the work of teenage girls and women, but kids in the Jarju compound always want to play at it.

"I started very badly," Ousman recalled. "The students were chanting 'A apple, B boy.' I just did the same. I didn't know what apple meant. It was very confusing."

The teacher, Njundu Fadera, had enrolled Ousman just a few weeks before the end of the school year. The final exam came quickly. When the results were announced Ousman was overjoyed because he saw the number 100 on his paper.

"I was shouting and dancing," he remembered. "But then someone told me that in the school's way of scoring, 100 was an almost complete failure. I cried. I had to repeat grade one."

The next year he finished second in his class. A girl named Aramata took first place, and she did the same in the next two years. In grade four Ousman finally caught up to Aramata. "I told her, 'If you ever beat me again, I will stop school,'" he said. During the rest of primary school and throughout middle school in the village, Ousman and Aramata were intense rivals. Sometimes one got first and the other second, sometimes the other way around. A boy named Amadou Touray often came in third.

In 2001, when Ousman was in grade eight in Salikenni, his father was unable to keep up with the fees. (Though small in primary school, the fees rose in higher grades.) The Gambia, like most countries in Africa south of the Sahara, could not afford to provide free public education to all children. (Today the country still struggles toward that goal.)

Ousman was exactly the kind of person my wife, Alison, and I had in mind when we launched the Salikenni Scholarship Fund (SSF) in 1996—a promising student who, without help, was likely to drop out of school because of the family's inability to pay. We took Ousman into the program in 2001.

The Salikenni village school only goes through grade nine. In order to attend high school students usually go to the metropolitan area of The Gambia, where they live with relatives. We sponsored Ousman to attend Nusrat Senior Secondary School in the suburbs of the capital city, Banjul.

Ousman ended his first year at Nusrat twelfth in his class. That was quite an achievement because Nusrat attracts many elite students from the urban area. But Ousman saw it as a defeat. "I said to myself, 'This place is quite different from Salikenni. I have to work harder.'" By grade twelve he had worked his way up to sixth position.

During high school Ousman lived in the compound of a relative. He had a room just big enough for one bed. He would sit on the bed and read his school books. But the compound was noisy, and it was hard to study there. Later, a man at a nearby youth center allowed him to study at night in the center's building. The man gave Ousman a key to be returned each morning.

In the spring of 2006, Ousman became the first in his family to finish high school. For the next three years SSF paid his tuition in a series of accounting courses at the Management Development Institute, a Gambian business college.

In 2010 Ousman was hired by the Gambian Interior Ministry as an accountant. While continuing to work there full-time he began courses at the University of The Gambia at night and on weekends, working for a bachelor's degree in accounting. SSF paid for his first year at the university. In March 2011 Ousman informed us by email that he had applied for and been granted a scholarship from the Gambian Treasury that would pay for the remaining years of his university study.

Ousman Jarju and his wife, Ndey, soon after their marriage in 2012.

In his email he expressed mixed emotions. He was happy that his portion of scholarship funds could now be used for other students, but sad to no longer be sponsored by "the program that brought me up." He said he would always be available to help SSF and its individual students, adding, "Please, I am still part of you." We assured him that would always be so.

Ousman followed what to most people would be an exhausting schedule. After a full day's work at the ministry he had just enough time to travel across town to attend university classes. Then he would go home and study late into the night.

In 2012 he married Ndey Dahaba, a gracious woman who is a graduate of an Arabic language high school. Their daughter, Sarata, was born on Christmas Day, 2012. In 2014 Ousman was promoted to senior accountant and attached to the Gambian passport office.

Ousman's father is now a full convert to education. Each of his six children younger than Ousman, five of them girls, over the years have been sent to school. The youngest, Abdou Karim, a boy, at the time of this writing is in grade two.

(For a long time I wondered whatever happened to Aramata, Ousman's childhood school rival. Then, while I was visiting Salikenni in 2013, she introduced herself as I bought candles at a local shop. Aramata told me she had completed high school and then taken two courses in operating computers. She had found a volunteer job in the town of Kerewan with a nonprofit organization that promoted girls' education. But the group had run out of funds and had suspended operations at least temporarily. Aramata had recently married Amadou Touray, the boy who often came in third in primary school rivalry. SSF sponsored Amadou through high school and in a series of courses in accounting at a local college. He is now a full-time accountant at NAWEC, the Gambian electric utility. Africa is such a small world, so full of surprises.)

Ousman remained active in SSF even after he no longer received our scholarship aid. He befriended and advised a number of our high school students who were struggling with their education. He helped graduates of the program look for jobs. He was a strong advocate of the idea that students who came up through the program should "give back" by tutoring and mentoring the younger students.

His leadership ability became increasingly apparent. When I visited The Gambia in November 2011, our then manager, Fatou Janneh, called a meeting of all our metropolitan area students and invited me to attend. She asked Ousman to chair the meeting. He began by asking for a moment of silent prayer, "each according to his tradition." He then pointed to several individual success stories. Three of the boys had recently achieved exceptional scores on their grade nine exams in Salikenni and were now in high schools in the urban area. Two of the girls had just entered the university. Ousman recognized one girl for a different reason: She had missed the grade nine pass mark by one point. With our financial support, she had just enrolled in a middle school in the urban area to repeat both grades eight and nine in order to make sure she would be well prepared for high school. Each of these students stood and received a round of applause. Ousman urged all the assembled students not to give up if they failed. He told them the story of how he once had to repeat grade one.

One theme that emerged clearly from that 2011 meeting was that the senior students were not only willing to give back to the program, but were also eager to participate in its management. Ousman told the group, "This program is entirely our own. We are one family. Let us help one another. We want this program to continue for a very long time. When we are no longer around, someone else will take over."

As it turned out, these sentiments would soon become a reality.

CHAPTER 2

"We" is Better than "I"

IN OCTOBER 2012, SSF came to a sudden, unexpected turning point. Fatou Janneh, a veteran English teacher and ministry of education official, who had been our manager in The Gambia since 2005, left with little advance notice to study for a master's degree in England under a Gambian government scholarship. Alison and I, as overall administrators of the program, phoned Ousman from our home in Vermont and asked him to take over as manager. He immediately accepted, provided he could recruit other higher-education students in the program to help him. He said the job was too big for one person and that they should work as a group. "I like the word 'we' better than 'I,'" he said. So, instead of getting just a new manager, we suddenly had an entire team.

On November 4, 2012, eight of our senior students—six men and two women—held an organizational meeting in the front room of Ousman's house in Fajikunda, in the heavily populated suburbs of Banjul, to make the new management arrangement official. For almost a year, this room became the Gambian headquarters of SSF. It was modestly furnished but clean. Some of the participants squeezed onto two couches with wooden arms and deep blue cushions, while others sat on white plastic chairs. The walls of the room were pale yellow. The ceiling was unpainted corrugated metal.

The floor was covered with linoleum, tan with dark red diamonds. A light blue curtain, hanging across the doorway to the courtyard outside, blew in and out with small puffs of breeze. Another blue curtain blocked the view into a bedroom, the only other room in the house.

The courtyard in front of the house was a large space, ringed by cement-block buildings with shallow-pitched metal roofs. Each building was a row of several contiguous houses, each with its own doorway to the courtyard.

Fajikunda is typical of dozens of neighborhoods in the suburbs of Banjul. The city proper is at the end of a narrow peninsula at the mouth of the Gambia River. Its growth, both commercial and residential, has sprawled over a wide area farther inland. A paved, four-lane, arterial street—its traffic often frighteningly fast, and just as often gridlocked—runs through many of these neighborhoods, which all look alike. Each neighborhood has a name, but there is nothing to indicate where one ends and the next begins. Both sides of this artery throb with commerce. There are big bank buildings, stores and shops of every possible kind and, at intervals, less-formal markets with narrow alleys running between tiny wooden shacks and open-air stalls. The sidewalks are always thronged with people. Gambians call the entire metropolitan area—Banjul and its suburbs—the Kombos, or often just Kombo. Nearly 60 percent of Gambians live in this urban area.

Residential Fajikunda lies one block behind the row of business establishments. Almost all the residential streets are unpaved. For block after block, when visiting the area, I walk on soft sand, stepping around areas of concrete rubble, passing walled compounds and a few very small shops that sell staples such as sugar in little plastic bags or vegetable oil by the cup. Little children shout "*tubab, tubab*," which means a white person. Some Gambians tell their children it is wrong to call out someone's skin color. But the children mean it in a friendly way. They rush up to shake hands. If I shake one hand I end up shaking a dozen. A little farther along, boys only a bit older take up the whole street playing football— the kind we in the United States call soccer. They never have a real football, often only a smaller children's ball, or sometimes an empty tin can. I have to be a bit careful walking through their game, because they play fast and with intensity. Young men sit idly in the shade in front of compounds and call out, "How's the day?" Other men and women, not idling but obviously on missions or errands of importance to them, walk along purposefully, exchanging only a nod or a quick word of greeting. Near Ousman's compound stands a beautiful mosque, glistening white with tall towers. Fajikunda is far from The Gambia's tourist areas along the oceanfront. I expect there are some, but I have never encountered another white face in Fajikunda.

After the students had found seats in his front room, Ousman formally opened the meeting with a moment of silent prayer. The participants held their hands out, palms up, moving their lips silently. All the students, including Ousman, were enrolled in the University of The Gambia or another higher-education institution in the country. One was just graduating from the university. All had reached this point in their education with assistance—at least part of the way—from the Salikenni Scholarship Fund.

Ousman was 28 at the time, muscular in body with an erect but relaxed posture, dark skin, a strong jaw, a high forehead and a broad grin. He is a man comfortable with leadership.

According to the minutes of the meeting, he began by calling for the "active involvement of everyone." "No one can do it alone," he told the group, "and in our quest to give back to the program what we have received, everyone ought to shoulder something." His opening remarks drew an enthusiastic response from the other students. Together they then created an organizational chart, parceling out responsibilities. They called themselves "the board." At the top of every page of the minutes, a header reads: "TOGETHER WE HAVE OUR FEET ON THE MOON."

A week after this organizational meeting, the board held a follow-up meeting to make more detailed plans. Present at the second meeting were two long-time American supporters of SSF—Mary Ann Roberts, a financial planner, and her husband, Bill Babcock, a lawyer, both of Alexandria, Virginia. They had been to The Gambia with me the previous year and had gone back for a second visit on their own.

Mary Ann wrote later that the students, one after another, "spoke at length about the importance of the program being locally managed by its own legacy members." They credited SSF "with providing their own education, a goal otherwise unattainable for them." "They are smart, educated, articulate, dedicated community development agents," she wrote. "They hope to one day be financial supporters themselves when they are established in their careers."

For a small, nonprofit organization like SSF, all this was a significant milestone. It meant that a core of educated students was being generated from within, students who were able and eager to take over as managers to keep the program going for future generations of boys and girls from the Salikenni area.

It meant also that SSF was coming close—at least in the area of local management—to something that all organizations working in poor countries seek: sustainability. Africa is strewn with the bones of development projects, started by well-intentioned outside donors, that failed because no one in the local community took the initiative to keep them going. On the edge of Salikenni village, just a few steps out into the grassland, stands a monument to a lack of sustainability. It's a windmill, a tall metal tower with fan-like blades on top and a fin to point the blades into the wind. It was built many years ago as part of an Italian aid project. The Italians wanted to create a fish processing plant so that the village could export fish from the river to markets in Banjul. They built several cement sheds near the river. The windmill, farther inland, was to provide fresh water through pipes to these sheds for the cleaning of fish. Ice was to be delivered in barges from Banjul, and the fish would go back on the same barges. The story, which I have heard from several people in the village, is that the Italians put a local man in charge of the windmill. He removed some of its parts and sold them. The Italians abandoned the project and went home. The windmill is still there. Once, when I walked by a few years ago, there was a strong breeze, and the blades were turning, turning, accomplishing nothing. Now, when I pass the spot, the blades are always stationary.

⚬•⊱⊰•⚬

There were nine members on the original board, including Ousman, as chairman and manager. Each member took on a specific area of responsibility—Salikenni student affairs, Kombos student affairs, working with SSF's female students at all school levels, communications (including writing meeting minutes), and two bookkeepers (one to keep financial records, the other to tally each student's academic performance).

The other board members and their responsibilities were:

- Amadou Njie—Kombos Student Affairs
- Abdoulie Bah—Salikenni Student Affairs
- Lamin B. Dibba—Salikenni Student Affairs (sharing the job with Abdoulie)
- Mariama Ceesay—Girls' Education
- Fatoumata M. Fatty—Girls' Education (sharing the job with Mariama)
- Modou Lamin Y. Darboe—Financial Bookkeeper
- Omar Jallow—Bookkeeper for Student Results
- Mustapha K. Darboe—Communications Officer

These board members deserve to be introduced individually because each has a different story—and because our students are the central characters in this book.

Amadou Njie—Kombos Student Affairs

Amadou is an amiable young man, always neatly dressed. At the time of the organizational meeting he was 24 and had just become the first of our scholarship students to complete a four-year undergraduate degree at the University of The Gambia.

Amadou joined SSF in 2002 when he was in grade eight at the Salikenni village school. In April of that year I visited the Njie compound, a cluster of whitewashed, cement-block buildings with corrugated metal roofs. Abdou Njie, Amadou's father, invited me into his house for a chat. The front room had white plaster walls, flaking away in some places, and a rough cement floor. The only furniture was a small wooden bench, on which Abdou motioned for me to sit. He sat on a big bag of rice.

Abdou wore a long, gray kaftan and a small, round cap, the traditional dress of elderly village men. He smiled broadly through his whiskers. As a local teacher translated from Mandinka, Abdou said he had two wives and sixteen children. He provided the older ones with almost no education; they were working on the family's farm plots outside the village. His son Ibrahim had stopped going to school after grade two. Another son, Lamin, had attended only Arabic school and was now selling used clothing in one of the metropolitan area markets. Four daughters were already married. Of these, only Tida had gone to school, but she had stopped after grade six.

But when it came to the younger children, Abdou's views had changed. He said he now wanted to educate some of them so that they could support the family in his old age. At the time of our conversation three children in the compound were attending the village school: Amadou, his younger brother, Ismaela, and Essa Samateh, who was a nephew of Abdou. Essa's father had "traveled" years earlier, leaving behind a wife and several small children. Abdou had taken the children into his compound and treated them as his own.

Stretching our rule against admitting more than one student in the same family to the SSF program, we had admitted two of these three schoolboys—Amadou and Essa.

When the three boys—Amadou, Essa and Ismaela—reached high school age, they lived together in a tiny room in Fajikunda. Because I wanted to know more about the housing conditions of our Kombos students, on one of my twice-a-year visits to The Gambia I asked Amadou and Essa to show me where they lived.

They led me on foot along dirt streets, turning left and right until I was totally lost. We entered a compound; a small, cement-block building with a corrugated metal roof and a row of corrugated metal doors stood at one end. Each of the metal doors was padlocked. The building resembled a small storage shed. I followed the boys to one door where Amadou removed the lock. "This is our house," he said.

Behind the door was a single room, perhaps ten-by-twelve feet. A double bed with a straw mattress took up most of the room, leaving only a narrow space at the foot and another along one side. There was a small table with books and papers stacked on it. There was a pile of neatly ironed clothing. Other clothing hung from nails along the once-whitewashed walls. The ceiling was made of bags stitched together, each labeled "Portland cement—Switzerland." The only daylight came from the open front door. There was no window, no electricity.

Amadou said that his older brother Lamin, the seller of used clothing, was paying the rent for the room. It was impossible to study there. The small courtyard out front belonged to families living in houses on the far side of it. They sat out there and talked and played loud music on battery-operated cassette players, and women cooked and did laundry. To study, the boys often went to the National Library in Banjul, which was next door to their high school.

We have had other students in the urban area whose housing conditions were similar or worse, and in some cases this seriously dragged down their academic performances. But Amadou and Essa always said, "We're managing."

Amadou finished high school in 2007. His final exam scores were not quite good enough for admission to the university. The university required five "credits" (a credit is a C or better) including English and math. Amadou got the five credits, but he failed math and got the lowest possible "pass" in English. Those two subjects are poorly taught in Gambian schools. That year, of the Gambian students in grade twelve who took the same exams, 67 percent failed English and 91 percent failed math.

However, the university accepted Amadou into an "access program" designed for students who showed promise but had trouble with some required subjects. Amadou went to classes in English and math for a year. He passed exams in each and in 2009 was fully admitted to the university, with a major in economics. (The university later abandoned the access program, but similar courses are now given by a number of private institutions.)

Throughout his four years at the university, Amadou continued to live in the same tiny room. He never once complained. When I asked him during several visits how he managed this, he would always reply, "I'm used to it."

In May of 2012 Amadou completed all the requirements for his degree. The next step was to find a job. He decided he would look for a job in one of the government economic ministries. His heart was set on getting a higher degree in his field. The university offered master's degrees only in history and French, but government agencies often sent employees who had worked for them for a few years to Europe or America for master's degrees or higher. "Private banks don't do that," he explained.

Amadou Njie—our first university graduate—and a very proud young man.

Immediately after receiving his documents from the university, Amadou filed his job application with the government's Personnel Management Office. Applicants are not permitted to apply directly to government agencies. The PMO is notorious for saying, "If we have an opening we will call you"—then silence. Amadou followed up several times, but the silence continued.

Amadou felt he was under acute pressure to find work. His family in Salikenni depended entirely on farming, but the most recent harvest season had been a disaster. The rains had stopped early, and the groundnut and rice crops had both largely failed. For several years, Amadou's father had supplemented his farming income by operating a small general merchandise shop near the main mosque in the village. But the shop had recently closed. Amadou said it "collapsed" due to "family pressure." Too much of the profit had been taken out to meet urgent financial needs of people in the extended family.

The only income earner in the Kombos to whom the family could look for help was Lamin, the seller of used clothing. But Lamin had a wife and three children of his own to support. Now that Amadou was a university graduate, Lamin no longer was willing to pay for the room in Fajikunda. "A lot is expected of me," Amadou said.

Resigning himself to a long wait for a government job, Amadou looked for other work and finally found a job teaching economics at a private high school, Charles Fowlis, on the main road to Banjul. This enabled him to find a better place to live and to begin sending money to his Salikenni family. It also gave him the time to take on a very big role in the management team—monitoring the progress of our students in the Kombos area, listening to their problems and helping to find solutions.

There are huge numbers of jobless young people in The Gambia. It is very difficult for someone with only a high school education to find a steady job. But Amadou said that university graduates with bachelor's degrees also have trouble finding work for which they have trained. "I have friends who graduated a year ago and are not yet employed," he told me.

Amadou is taking the frustration of job hunting in stride. "I believe I am on the right track," he said. "I have seen that the best way to alleviate poverty from your family is through education."

On March 15, 2014, the university held its formal graduation ceremony. Amadou stood tall and smiling in a cap and gown and officially received his degree. He wrote us in an email: "I vividly remember the day when I collected the admission form from the University of The Gambia. I never thought I would make it to the end of the road because of so many challenges. But with hard work, determination, support from friends, family members, enemies, and more importantly my sponsors, I have finally reached the end of the road successfully."

———◆•▪•◆———

Abdoulie Bah—Salikenni Student Affairs

Abdoulie was 22 at the time of the organizational meeting and was in his third year at the university, working toward a bachelor's degree in accounting. He is of medium height and slender build with a long, narrow face. He comes from Dobo, a small village about an hour's walk from Salikenni. It is one of several nearby villages whose children attend the Salikenni school for part of their education and are therefore eligible for the SSF program. Dobo has a primary school for grades one through six. But for grades seven through nine about 40 of its children walk the narrow sand road to and from Salikenni every day. They travel in bunches of five or ten, the boys in their uniforms of dark blue shorts and white shirts, the girls in black skirts and white blouses.

I first met Abdoulie in March 2008, during one of my visits to Salikenni. One evening, Sankung Daffeh, then principal of the Salikenni school, brought Abdoulie and his father, Amadou, to the room where I was staying. Amadou is smaller in build than his son but with the same long face and strong jaw. We talked a long time, with Daffeh translating for me. The room grew darker, until we could hardly see each other.

Daffeh said that Amadou was the head of a Dobo compound with about nine people, including his two wives, their children and various relatives. He made most of his living by tending cattle owned by others, but he had a few cattle of his own. At one time he owned five bulls, but in recent years he had sold them one by one to pay school fees for several children, including Abdoulie.

He had just sold his last bull to pay Abdoulie's tuition for grade ten at Nusrat Senior Secondary School in the suburbs of Banjul. Amadou was also a part-time farmer, but his recent groundnut crop had failed. The harvest was not enough even to provide seeds for the following year, and he still owed money for the last batch of seeds. He was very worried that Abdoulie would have to drop out of school at the end of the current year.

We admitted Abdoulie to our program in grade eleven for the 2008–09 academic year. (This was one of several exceptions we have made over the years to our normal policy of bringing new students in at grade seven.)

Abdoulie completed high school in June 2010. His results on the exam that students throughout the country take at the end of grade twelve more than met the requirements for admission to the university. But rather than enter the university that September he chose to wait for the January 2011 intake. He wanted to spend some time in Dobo helping his family with the farming. He also wanted to give math lessons to some of the younger students who lived in Dobo. Our manager at the time, Fatou Janneh, suggested that maybe he could also tutor some of our sponsored students in Salikenni, and he quickly agreed.

For more than a month in the fall of 2010, Abdoulie lived in Salikenni from Monday through Thursday and held math classes each night in the school library for SSF students in grades seven through nine. On weekends he walked back to Dobo to help with the farm work and to tutor other Dobo students who were not sponsored by SSF. This was the beginning of what has become a growing trend in our program: senior students going to Salikenni as their schedules permit to tutor our younger students there, or in other cases tutoring our high school students in the metropolitan area. (Mariama Ceesay, our first student in medical school, joined Abdoulie in Salikenni that fall. She taught the students English for one hour each evening while he taught math for one hour.)

I attended several of the tutoring classes in the library in Salikenni during that fall. Because rural electrification had recently come to Salikenni, we had equipped the library with two overhead rows of energy-saving bulbs, which gave off a pale, harsh light, and also attracted swarms of mosquitoes through the open doorway. The classes were punctuated by the sound of all of us slapping mosquitoes. With a stub of chalk and a piece of string, Abdoulie drew arcs on the blackboard, demonstrating how to work with angles. He didn't own a watch, but he had an uncanny sense of time. During each lesson that I attended, at one point he would walk over to me and whisper, "What time is it?" It was always exactly ten minutes before the class was scheduled to end.

On another occasion I visited Abdoulie in his family compound in Dobo. Wuyeh Keita, another of our scholarship students, then in grade nine in Salikenni, walked with me from Salikenni to Dobo early one Saturday morning. The road is just two tracks in the sand, or more accurately three tracks because much of the traffic along it consists of horse and donkey carts. The animals make a light track in the center, while the wheels make deeper ruts on each side. We walked past fields on either side where groundnuts and millet and corn were growing.

Dobo is smaller than Salikenni. Many of its residents, including Abdoulie's family, are of the Fula tribe, while most people in Salikenni are Mandinkas. The Fulas are traditionally cattle raisers. Mandinkas are mainly farmers.

Abdoulie welcomed us into his compound. The main building was rectangular, made of dark, red-brown mud bricks with doorways to several apartments. There were also two small mud-brick houses of traditional Fula design—round with conical thatched roofs. Surrounding the compound was a fence made of sticks and reeds that had been woven together, except for a wide entrance with no gate.

One of the small round houses belonged to Abdoulie; he invited Wuyeh and me inside. The house had just one circular room that was about six paces across. The curving wall was bare mud-brick. Blackish timbers supported a tan thatch ceiling that rose in a tall cone. A low half-wall, also mud-brick, created an alcove. It was barely big enough for a small bed, which was covered by a red and white checkered cloth. The dirt floor of the main area had been swept very clean and smooth. A few items of clothing hung on nails around the walls.

Because of the height of the roof and the thickness of the thatch, the house felt pleasantly cool, though outside, the midmorning sun was already giving off an oppressive heat. There were no windows, but thin curtains that hung at two open doorways let in plenty of light and air.

The three of us sat on plastic chairs around a small table draped with a blue and white checkered cloth. Abdoulie placed a large plastic bowl with a plastic lid on the table in front of us. On top of the lid a pile of ground millet had been carefully placed. It looked like brownish sand. Abdoulie gave each of us a large plastic spoon with a bowl-like end. He picked up the lid with one hand and poured some of the powdery millet into the bowl, stirring with a spoon in his other hand. His motions were slow and careful, and the expression on his face showed concentration and a bit of pride, as though this were a royal dinner. We all dipped our spoons into the common bowl.

Milk and millet are staple foods in Dobo. The village is awash with milk. Dobo is far from the river, and its land is more suitable to growing millet than rice. A breakfast of fresh milk and millet is an unforgettable experience. The milk is so fresh and warm that I sense the nearness of the cow. Millet doesn't mix with milk but sinks to the bottom. The trick is to dip the spoon deeply enough to come up with both millet and milk. Too much millet feels like a mouthful of sand. Milk alone is not a meal. The right proportion is delicious and satisfies hunger.

"When I was a small boy, seven or eight, I raised sheep," Abdoulie said. His father had given him a female sheep and goat. Eventually he had about ten sheep and several goats. He sold one from time to time to earn a little money.

His schooling began with two years studying Arabic and the Koran in a class taught by a Dobo religious leader. He entered grade one at the age of nine in the government school in Bani, another village relatively close to Salikenni. Bani was chosen because, at the time, that was where the cattle were. His family often drove their cattle to the Bani area during the dry months of the year and then returned to Dobo with the cattle each rainy season to engage in farming.

"I had to repeat grade one," Abdoulie recalled, "because I had started it very late in the school year. That made me try harder the next year."

Each morning during his middle school years, Abdoulie ate some milk and millet in Dobo and left at 7 a.m. to walk to the Salikenni school. When his classes ended at 2 p.m. he walked home and went to the family's farms to do whatever chores were needed—weeding, harvesting or tending cattle. He spent a lot of time milking cows. After 6 p.m. he would go home, bathe from a bucket, have dinner and then study by candlelight. He was an avid soccer player during those years, although he gave up the sport in high school because his studies were more demanding.

In the second year of his accounting studies at the university, Abdoulie began to think about how he would support himself and his family once he graduated. While most of our students pin their hopes on finding a job, Abdoulie developed a different strategy. He decided that during his upcoming three-month summer break, he would return to Dobo, continue his tutoring and continue helping on the family farms. But he would also do some farming on his own to earn money. He would repeat this in future summers. He also was considering a possible plan to buy groundnuts from Dobo area farmers when the price was low, store the crop and then resell it to the government or to traders from Senegal later in the year when prices would be higher. He estimated he could clear 10,000 dalasis ($300 to $400 depending on the exchange rate) each summer. When he graduated he would have enough capital to start a small business.

"That's my dream," he told me. "The government cannot do all these things for the people. The people have to help themselves. I don't want to look for a job. I want to start a business and employ other people and move the country forward."

During the 2013 growing season, as he began his final year at the university, Abdoulie had saved 5,000 dalasis (then about $170) from his part-time farming business. He borrowed a similar amount from a bank. With this combined capital, he planted groundnuts, maize and coos, hired some local workers, rented some simple equipment, and by the end of the season he had earned enough profit to start the following year on a larger scale. He was looking for outside investors to enable him to further increase production.

Abdoulie has since returned to Salikenni and Dobo several times to tutor. At the organizational meeting of the board he spoke out strongly on the need for all the senior students to work together. "We should work as a family and not as separate people working to achieve different aims and objectives," he said.

Lamin B. Dibba—Salikenni Student Affairs

Lamin, 18 at the time of the organizational meeting, served as a member of the original board during its first year. He is a strong-bodied young man with a very broad smile. In November 2012 Lamin had just finished high school with superlative grades, and he was about to enter the university with a major in accounting. He had been in our program since grade seven.

Lamin is the son of Bakary Dibba, a Salikenni farmer and fisherman who is deaf and does not speak, but who always greets me with a powerful bear hug when I visit his compound. This family has a particularly strong regard for education. Lamin was the first in the immediate family to go to high school; his three younger brothers were all in school. An uncle, Saikou Dibba, years earlier had managed to finish high school and then trained as a teacher. He taught for many years in Gambian schools and then became a senior education officer at the Ministry of Basic and Secondary Education. Since coming to the urban area for high school, Lamin had lived with Saikou Dibba in a comfortable suburban house.

Regarding his ambition to qualify for the university, Lamin left nothing to chance. Months before his grade twelve exam, he paid the fee to take a private version of the same exam as a warm-up. He got three A's, four B's and a C, so at that point he had already met the university's admission requirements. But Lamin was sure he could do better on the regular exam. He told me that what he really wanted was to go to a university in the United States or United Kingdom. I explained that SSF had never provided a scholarship abroad. "What would it take?" Lamin asked. "Suppose I got nine A's?"

"If you get nine A's call me," I said. As it turned out, he got five A's, three B's and a C, which was spectacular, but he didn't press his request for a scholarship abroad.

Lamin has strong Muslim convictions. His uncle recommended he major in accounting at the university. But Lamin worried that accountants must deal with interest and this would conflict with his religion. He would find another branch of commerce. Others among our senior students advised him that accounting was a surer route to a job, and he did finally choose that as his major.

He entered the university in January 2013. In September of that year, as he was just starting his second semester, Lamin suddenly got his wish to study abroad. He received a letter offering him a full scholarship to study for an undergraduate degree in economics at Abant Izzet Baysal University in Turkey. "I was not so sure it was true," he told us in an email. He took the letter to the Turkish embassy and was told, yes, it was true. But the embassy said that to meet the deadline for the program he would have to get his visa the very next morning. He did. A few hours later he was on his way to Dakar, where he boarded a plane for Turkey.

A few days later he emailed us to say he had arrived safely and was enrolled in the university in the town of Bolu in an area of forests and mountains in western Turkey. His first year would be spent learning the Turkish language. "I am told," he wrote, "that it won't take me more than five months to speak it."

———◆◆◆———

Mariama Ceesay—Girls' Education

SSF has always stressed equal education opportunity for boys and girls. The job of mentoring our female students, both in Salikenni and the metropolitan area, is an important one in our program. Many of our girls have a more difficult struggle with education than the boys. (See Chapter 7.) Mariama was 21 at the time of the organizational meeting and in her second year at the University of The Gambia Medical School. She was the first of our students of either gender to be admitted there. The medical school is a seven-year program.

Mariama did not grow up in Salikenni. Her parents lived there but moved to the Banjul area before she was born. She grew up in Latrikunda, which today is a crowded, bustling metropolitan suburb. Mariama says that when she was a young girl the neighborhood still had open spaces and many mango and orange trees. She attended the local government middle school, which she remembers as understaffed and lacking enough textbooks. "But if there was no teacher and you could find books, and if you were willing to learn, you could do your best and get into secondary school," she once told me.

In 2008, when she was in the grade eleven science program at Nusrat Senior Secondary School, we added her to the scholarship program on the recommendation of our then manager, Fatou Janneh, who said that Mariama was a student of great promise but needed assistance because her family was not wealthy. Fatou also felt that Mariama would be a strong role model for the younger girls in the program.

After Mariama finished high school SSF paid for her first year in medical school, but then she applied for and received a Gambian government scholarship for the remainder of her medical training.

Early in her second year in medical school, I visited Mariama at her family home in Latrikunda. She suggested we meet at the Latrikunda garage, because her house would be difficult to find in a neighborhood where few streets have signs and few houses have numbers. In The Gambia a garage is not a building for cars. It's a place where several streets intersect and long lines of small yellow taxis and rickety vans wait for full loads of passengers. It is jammed with people moving in every direction—on foot, on bicycles, others pushing wheelbarrows, others with large bundles on their heads, women in traditional African gowns, others in smart western dresses, laborers in work clothes, and school children in neatly ironed uniforms.

Mariama appeared out of the crowd dressed all in black—a long black robe and a tight-fitting black head covering that left only the oval of her face showing. Many of the girls in SSF wear a head covering (*hijab* in Arabic), but some of them do not. Coming from the Salikenni area, all are Muslims. Their choice of dress depends on whether they and their families are more conservative or less so. None of our girls veil their faces.

Mariama led me along several streets and around corners to a gate similar to many others in the neighborhood. Inside the gate was a neat and clean compound with a large vegetable garden on one side and on the other, a white masonry building with several apartments. We entered one of these and sat in the parlor, which was comfortably but not expensively furnished with upholstered chairs.

Mariama introduced me to her mother, Hawa Kassama, who was also clad in religious black; her grandmother, who wore a colorful, traditional Gambian long dress; a sister, Fatoumata; and another sister, Binta, who was also at the university, studying management and information systems under a government scholarship. Mariama said her father, Momodou Ceesay, sold used clothing at the Banjul market; her mother was unemployed.

Mariama told me that she hoped to specialize in gynecology because she has seen the medical problems of Gambian women. "I want to work with them and help them," she said.

Though she didn't grow up in Salikenni, she has shown a strong commitment to the village. Some of her relatives still live there, and she stays with them during her periodic visits to conduct tutoring classes in the Salikenni library. During one of those classes, which I attended, Mariama focused on reading comprehension. This is an area of weakness for many of our students, but it is always part of the grade nine exam that determines eligibility for high school. Mariama had the students read a passage, and then asked them questions about it. She urged them to stop and think, "What is the writer of this paragraph trying to tell me?" She also gave them some practical tips on how to answer questions on the exam: Always write the answer in complete sentences or the examiners will make a lot of red marks. Never copy verbatim from the paragraph. Put your answers in your own words.

Mariama is a strong defender of Gambian students getting a Gambian education. To students who say they would get a better education if they could find a scholarship in the United States or Europe, she replies: "The University of The Gambia is a young institution. It opened in 1999. Its medical school is even newer. If everybody says they don't want to go to the university, how will it grow and gain respect in the world? Even Harvard started from somewhere."

<hr>

Fatoumata M. Fatty—Girls' Education

Fatoumata was 20 at the time of the organizational meeting and was in her second year at the university, studying for a bachelor's degree in accounting. "Fatty" is an old and quite frequent Mandinka surname, which should be pronounced FAH-tee. Fatoumata is small, poised and self-confident. She grew up in Ba Santo, the poorest section of Salikenni. Her parents were Salikenni farmers, but they moved to Banjul when Fatoumata was a little girl, leaving her to be raised in the village by her grandmother,

Sisanding Kolley. Her father became a stevedore at the Banjul port.

Fatoumata joined SSF in 2005, one of twelve students we admitted that year in grade seven at the Salikenni school. She was the only one of the twelve to reach the university. SSF's annual report from 2005 includes her picture, a smiling young girl, wearing a headscarf. The caption reads: "Fatoumata is always busy at home with the traditional work of girls. She cooks over a wood fire. She washes clothes in basins, goes to the public tap to draw a big bucket of water and carries it home on her head, and pounds grains into usable form. But her grandfather, Abdou Fatty, says that now that she is moving up in school he will make sure she does not have so much household work that she cannot study or will be late to school."

When Fatoumata was about to start high school, Fatou Janneh wanted to put her into St. Joseph's school for girls in Banjul. But St. Joseph's would not allow girls to cover their heads, and Fatoumata declined to go there. Instead she enrolled in Muslim Senior Secondary School, a big institution, which is part of the government education system, in the heart of Banjul. It has large classes. Its students are on their own to sink or swim. Some of our students have failed there. But Fatoumata quietly made it through grade twelve, never reporting a problem, never asking for anything, and ending up with a grade twelve exam score of five A's, two B's and a C. She entered the university in 2011. We paid for her first year there. The next year she was given a Gambian government scholarship that paid for the remaining years of her university program.

I visited Fatoumata and her family in 2012 in their home in a residential neighborhood in Banjul called Tobacco Road. It consists of block after block of unpaved streets. Many of the compound walls and buildings on either side are in obvious need of repair. Open drainage ditches containing a foul, dark liquid run through the area. In many places, pedestrians must step over them.

Fatoumata guided me on foot for several blocks to an iron gate and then up a short walkway to a small, one-story house. The family was dressed up for my visit. Her mother, Fatoumata Marong, wore a light blue African dress and matching headscarf. Her father, Masanneh Fatty, looked stylish in a freshly ironed shirt. The front room of the house was spotlessly clean. There were several upholstered chairs. The walls were decorated with rows of family photographs in frames. Fatoumata wore a light pink dress and a black headscarf. She said her father worked at the port only occasionally now. Her mother earned a little money at home making powdered soap, which she put into little plastic bags and sold to women in the neighborhood.

Fatoumata said that ever since primary school she had had a clear goal: "I must go to the university." She said her grandmother encouraged her in this ambition.

When she graduates from the university, Fatoumata wants to find a job as an accountant. "I want to work so that I can help my family," she said. After working a few years, she said, she might look for a government scholarship and get a master's degree.

Modou Lamin Y. Darboe—Financial Bookkeeper

Lamin, as everyone calls him, was 20 at the time of the organizational meeting and in his third year at the university, majoring in economics. "This is a dream for us," he said. "We have been aspiring to manage this program ourselves. We will succeed."

Lamin is tall and very slender. He did not grow up in Salikenni. His father, Yusupha Darboe, originally from Salikenni, was a teacher. He worked in a succession of schools and took Lamin with him to each new assignment. In the 2002–03 academic year Yusupha was posted to the Salikenni school, and Lamin was enrolled in grade six there. At the end of that school year, Lamin was one of a group of students selected by a village committee to receive SSF scholarships. (We no longer use the committee system of selection.) Shortly before the start of classes, Yusupha was posted to another village. Lamin went with him, and our scholarship followed him. We continued to sponsor him through middle school and high school. When he was in grade twelve his father died. His exam results that year were good except for English and math. At SSF expense he spent a year in the university access program studying those two subjects and, in 2010, was admitted to the university.

"Without SSF I would have been a dropout," Lamin once told me. He has given much back to the program as a volunteer. He has often worked as an assistant to an outside math teacher hired by SSF to tutor our metropolitan area students in weekend classes. And when that teacher was unavailable, Lamin often conducted those classes himself.

Omar Jallow—Bookkeeper for Student Results

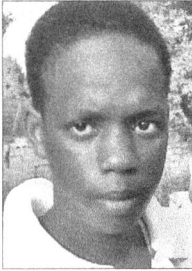

Omar, 19 at the time, was unable to attend the organizational meeting of the board, but his name was added a short time later as a second bookkeeper, responsible for tallying the results of each student in their schools. He is also an all-purpose volunteer, willing to take on any chore at any time.

Omar comes from the village of Dobo. His father, Naibelly Jallow, is a tall, distinguished-looking man, a farmer, very active in Dobo affairs. Omar is slight in build and quiet. His narrow face usually bears a serious expression. We brought him into the SSF program in 2009 because his grade nine exam results were quite good but the family was very poor and unlikely to be able to afford high school.

He did well at Masroor Senior Secondary School, in the far suburbs of Banjul. He wanted to be a doctor, but was torn between that ultimate goal and the need to start helping to support his family soon. The medical school in The Gambia takes seven years. "I am the first to go to school," he told us, "and my parents might need assistance."

His father urged him to pursue the goal of medicine anyway. However, the medical school did not accept him because of one bare pass, in chemistry. He could have spent a year in a private access program to improve that grade, as several of our students have done. But he chose instead to enroll in a four-year program at the university to earn a bachelor of science degree in nursing. He began that program in September 2012.

Mustapha K. Darboe—Communications Officer

 Mustapha is an outgoing young man in his early 20s with a burning ambition to become a journalist. He has been in our program since 2001 when he was in grade seven in the Salikenni school. Nothing about him aroused our attention until he was in high school, when we began to notice that he had a literary streak. Our then manager, Fatou Janneh, as part of her weekend English tutoring class, would often ask our metropolitan area students to write short essays, and she would pass some of these on to us.

One week's topic was "How I Spent *Tabaski*." *Tabaski* is the Gambian name for the Muslim holiday *Eid al-Adha*. It is the biggest holiday of the year. It celebrates the story, found in Muslim, Christian and Jewish holy books, of Abraham's willingness to kill his own son, Ismail, to show his loyalty to God, and how God substituted, at the last moment, a ram for the slaughter. In Salikenni members of extended families from far away gather for this holiday. Everyone has, or hopes to have, new clothes. Rams are slaughtered, and everyone enjoys the feast.

Most of the essays contained a minimum of description: "I went home, took bath, greeted my family." Mustapha's was lyrical: "I wake up at 7:30 a.m., the brighter sun smiling in the east, the sky in its lovely look blue like an ocean water, the air blowing sweeter than soul."

He once sent us a poem entitled "The Dream that Realized." Its final lines read:

Behold, the man of people, smart dressed, uniting the masses

I have a dream, the mouths opened, all eyes red, the ears eager to hear, plain papers in hands, because known for righteousness

One day this nation will rise up and bring out the true meaning of its creed, we hold this truth to be self evident, that all men are created equal.

Revolution start in 2008 and choose Barack solution Obama.

It was clear to us that Mustapha was a poet trapped in extreme grammatical dysfunction. After graduating from high school he sent us a letter in longhand, in which he declared: "My goal is seeing myself a world classic journalist, writing powerful book, and interviewing powerful people in powerful radio and television." His high school results did not meet the university's admission standards, but over the next several years SSF sponsored Mustapha in a series of journalism courses in local training schools. In 2013 he earned a graduate degree in journalism from Stratford College of Management in The Gambia. Along the way, Alison gave him an informal English grammar course by email, in which he filled in the correct word in a sentence or sent her brief passages, which she edited and returned to him.

As a member of the management team Mustapha has been responsible for keeping the minutes of meetings. His command of English has much improved. His style is image-laden, almost reminiscent of Charles Dickens. His account of the board's second meeting, a week after it was organized, began: "In the scorching heat of the 17th of November, Saturday afternoon, journeyed the senior students of the Salikenni Scholarship Fund, to gather in the house of the new manager, Ousman Jarju, to talk about the challenges that lie ahead in their new task of managing the program."

———◆◆◆◆———

Five months after the management board was formed, Ousman and I, along with the SSF librarian, Fatou Darboe, traveled together from Fajikunda to Salikenni, where we planned to meet with our students and their parents. On visits to The Gambia over the years, I have always avoided means of travel common among tourists or people associated with wealthier organizations—the tourist taxis, the shiny SUVs—and instead have moved about by the same transportation systems that ordinary Gambians use.

So one morning the three of us stood on the side of the main thoroughfare, waiting for a commercial van with three empty seats bound for Banjul. Many full vans flew by us. These vehicles are decrepit, standard passenger vans. Their cushioned seats have been replaced by hard, narrow benches so they can carry about 15 people. They follow set routes, which together form a network as efficient as a modern urban subway and bus system. But they are not marked, and there is no transit map. You have to know the routes. Each van has a driver and an *aprendi*, a young man who collects the fares and who leans out of an open window shouting the vehicle's destination. He opens the sliding side door when the van stops to let passengers on or off. He bangs on the outside of the van to tell the driver to start moving again. Then he often has to run to catch up with the already-moving vehicle. Small yellow taxis also ply the same routes, but they can hold at most four passengers at a time, and they often charge a bit more. The main problem with this transit system is that there are not enough vans and group taxis. During the morning rush hour, every block of every main street is lined by dozens, sometimes hundreds, of people—men, women and school children in their uniforms—waiting for a place in a van. Few of them will get to work or school on time. Some large employers, including the government agency where Ousman works, operate their own buses to get their employees to work.

But we had set out well after the rush hour and we quickly found a van with empty seats. Once you are inside a vehicle the trip into Banjul goes very fast. We disembarked at the open-air Banjul garage and walked about 15 minutes through the city, carrying our bags, to the ferry terminal. The terminal is always jammed with passengers and stevedores with goods piled on pushcarts. Vendors walk about carrying armloads of sandals, belts, underwear or flip-flops. Men and women with bundles on their heads push and shove their way onto the ferry's main deck, squeezing between big trucks, some still maneuvering into place.

The ferry ride across the wide mouth of the Gambia River to Bara takes about 40 minutes. Bara is a town of extreme squalor. It is the gateway for road transport to Dakar in Senegal and the entry point into the rural and generally very poor North Bank region of The Gambia.

The Gambia is a tiny country—its population in 2011 was 1.8 million—on the sweeping curve of Africa's great bulge into the Atlantic Ocean. The entire country is 270 miles long and nowhere more than 30 miles wide. It is really just the Gambia River and some of the banks on either side. Except for a short section of Atlantic coast, it is entirely surrounded by a much larger country, Senegal. On a map it looks like a splinter stuck into the hide of its big neighbor. These boundaries were inherited from the nineteenth century, when European powers carved up Africa into colonies, paying little attention to ethnic distribution or regional economics. The British took control of the river and its port. The French colonized a large surrounding area, then known as French West Africa, with its capital at Dakar. The British called their little colony The Gambia. When the country became independent, peacefully, in 1965, "The" became part of its official name. Today the official language of The Gambia—the language of government, banking, education and large business—is English. In Senegal it is French. For local people this language barrier is not very important, because their local languages, Wolof and Mandinka and many others, are spoken in both countries. Life expectancy at birth in The Gambia is 58 years. The national income per person is around $500 a year. Forty-eight percent of the population lives below the country's official poverty line.

At the open air Bara garage a hundred or so vans and buses and other vehicles are parked in jumbled rows, waiting for passengers. Everyone is shouting. Drivers and their *aprendi* insist that you join their vehicles whether you are going their way or not. We made our way through the confusion to a certain unmarked spot in the garage where the vans to Salikenni always park. In Mandinka these vans are called *katsumbaru*. They are a bit larger than the ones that whiz about Banjul and its suburbs. Each has a railing around its roof to hold cargo, which can include live sheep or goats or bags of farm produce. Most of the vans are brightly decorated, and many have the Arabic phrase *Alhamdulillah*, which means praise to God, painted in large capital letters across their front ends.

Vans at the Bara garage don't move until they are full, which can mean a long wait, as the author, on many trips, found out.

The vans don't budge until they are full. Sometimes the wait can be an hour until the next ferry brings more passengers. If the van is still not full, everyone has to wait for yet another ferry and sometimes for the one after that. We were lucky to get the last three seats in the morning van to Salikenni. As vans move out, the garage is seized by a honking, shouting semi-gridlock. This is made worse by the fact that there are always some vehicles with dead batteries. The other drivers jump out of their own vans to help push.

During my first few visits to The Gambia, the highway that runs eastward through the North Bank region was unpaved—hazardous at best and verging on impassable during the rainy season. Today it is blacktop. A second ferry, which we had to take across the Kerewan River, has been replaced by a bridge, built by the government of Taiwan. (The Gambia is one of four African countries that officially recognize Taiwan as the Republic of China and perhaps as a result of this has received substantial economic aid from the Taiwanese government.)

The highway runs across an almost flat plain of grassland, brush, small cultivated fields and a scattering of trees. The most majestic of the trees are the baobabs, with trunks as fat as elephants and colored the same gray, but with spindly upper branches and dark, oblong hanging fruit often used for making juices. We were traveling in the dry season, and the landscape to the horizon was brown. With the coming of the rains it would become green and beautiful.

Stray cows, goats and dogs wandered across the road. The driver steered around them. We flew past horse carts and donkey carts, motorbikes, bicycles, and past people walking along the roadsides. More than once on my trips all the passengers have had to get out while the crew changed a blown tire. Thankfully, not this time.

The highway passes many villages. We stopped often to let passengers off and on. At many stops, the young *aprendi* climbed onto the van's roof to unload cargo into the outstretched arms of people waiting on the ground. After about forty miles we came to Dobo—the home village of our senior student board member, Abdoulie Bah. There we turned off the highway onto a narrow sand road that runs south through the dry countryside. On both sides we saw blackened fields that had recently been burned off to prepare for the next growing season. We passed a herd of several dozen long-horned cattle, tended by a small boy. After about five miles we approached an area of trees, through which we caught glimpses of corrugated roofs. A moment later we were in the lanes of Salikenni, moving carefully past pedestrians and playing children, navigating close to jagged metal fences. We passed the youth center and the main mosque and stopped near the central *banteba*, where the old men interrupted their talk of politics long enough to give us a smile and a wave of welcome. For us it was time to get work. There were students and parents to meet and, inevitably, problems to solve.

CHAPTER 3

"Can You Pay My School Fees?"

I FIRST VISITED SALIKENNI in 1989 as an economics reporter interested in village development. The selection of this village was purely accidental. After nearly four decades of working for the *Washington Daily News* and *United Press International*, I was now working for *The Washington Times*.

Unlike my previous employers, the *Times* had money to burn; it sent me on a two-month trip to a half dozen countries in both East and West Africa. My last stop was Banjul, where I made an appointment to interview Malang Camara of the Gambian Department of Community Development. For several years that agency had been encouraging rural villages to set up village development committees (VDCs). The concept was fairly new at the time, but since then has become widely accepted. The idea was to encourage local communities to take charge of their own development rather than have outside donors tell them what their needs were. The earlier model had resulted in many failures in Africa.

"Under the old system," Camara told me, "a foreign donor or a nongovernmental organization would go into a village and say, 'We are going to dig wells,' or, 'Here is an irrigation canal. Here are some tractors. Now this is what we want you to do.' The project would run for a few years and then the donors would go away. Everything would stop. The wells would cave in. The canals would go dry. The tractors would break down. If you go into one of those villages today, people will tell you, 'When the white man was here you should have seen the things we had.'"

Under the new approach, villagers were encouraged to be their own development planners. Community development field workers would go to a village and encourage people there to hold one or more meetings to discuss their problems among themselves. Camara said that the message of the field workers was: "You are the ones who have to solve your problems. We can help you make contacts with outside agencies and groups that can give you some assistance. But you are the ones who have to decide what your problems are and how you are going to solve them. You are the ones who will have to organize the solutions, and you are the ones who will have to do most of the work."

If a village decided to form a village development committee, its members would receive training in organization, management of programs, bookkeeping and communications. The committee then would be urged to set its own priorities and figure out how much these would cost and which ones were most feasible.

I asked Camara if he could suggest a village with a VDC that I could visit to see how it worked. He put me in touch with Save the Children USA, which at that time was one of several non-governmental organizations (NGOs) taking part in this program, each in a different area. Save the Children recommended that I visit Salikenni.

I rented an old Jeep and drove it onto, then off the ferry. I drove along the North Bank highway, which was then unpaved, with stretches of soft sand. Along the route, people asked for rides. I invited them to pile in, happy to have them for company and to tell me where I was at a given moment.

I turned off the highway onto a narrow sand road at a small village called Bani. The dirt road from Bani and the one from Dobo both lead to Salikenni but from different directions. In those days, coming from Bani, the entrance to Salikenni was almost majestic. The road there was of reddish sand, and it curved to the left just before the village. On the right-hand side, there was a row of immense baobab trees that followed the curve of the road. Probably no one had planted them there. More likely, there had once been many more baobabs, and farmers had cut down the ones in the fields, leaving only those along the road. On the left side of the road there was a row of tall mango trees, with a field behind

Many Gambian villages have women's community gardens. This one is in Mandori, near Salikenni. Women grow vegetables for their families and to sell at a nearby market town.

them. Most of the baobabs were later cut down to make room for an electric power line; the mangos are still there. In the spring it is acceptable for passers-by to pick one or two of the fruit. When the low-hanging fruit is gone, boys climb the trees, or they stand in the road and, with impressive accuracy, throw stones to sever the thin stems from which the mangos hang in the trees.

On that first visit I stopped the Jeep to take in the view—the reddish road, the stately trees, the green fields behind them, and just ahead the white buildings of the village school. I drove to the school and immediately was surrounded by excited children, and, as I later learned was typical, I shook dozens of hands.

Fodayba Danso, the chairman of the Village Development Committee, was a sprightly, middle-aged man, wearing a long kaftan. Mainding Touray, a smiling woman in a colorful African robe, was vice-chairman and was also called the "lady president." They showed me two of their projects, both largely completed. When Save the Children first asked the committee to list its priorities, the members had no hesitation naming the most important one: The village needed to grow more food. The first project was to clear about a hectare of unused land that had become overgrown with brush. Save the Children provided cutlasses and axes. The villagers provided the labor, and they cleared an area where the women now were growing rice. The second project was to provide village women with a place to grow vegetables during the long, dry season. An area was cleared and fenced. Wells were dug for irrigation. The garden grew. It is still in use today.

On that first visit, I spent only a few hours in the village. On the way back, I noticed that gasoline was dripping from the Jeep's tank. I stopped and found a mechanic who plugged the hole with a twig and, I think, chewing gum. That was the only time I rented my own vehicle to travel to Salikenni. I have since always used the commercial vans.

———•◆••◆•———

I visited The Gambia a second time in 1991 in the course of another trip to several African countries, this time as a freelance reporter. (In the trade, this is a well-known euphemism for unemployed.) I made my way by commercial transport to Kerewan, a medium-sized town and a seat of district government on the North Bank highway on the way to Salikenni. I met Kebba Ceesay, a community development assistant, based in Kerewan, and told him I hoped to visit Salikenni again and maybe stay for a week or so. He drove me there in his truck and introduced me to Buba Bojang, a young agricultural extension worker then based in the village.

When we arrived, without advance notice, Ceesay told Bojang about my vague plan to spend some time there. "No problem!" Bojang replied. He could easily find me a place to stay. On second thought he would give me his own house and he would sleep elsewhere. No, he wouldn't have it any other way. His house would be much more convenient. I could stay as long as I wished. He would arrange meetings with anyone I wanted to see and, when necessary, would act as translator. He was my host for four days; this was my first immersion into village life.

Bojang's compound was composed of three long, one-level buildings, built of cement blocks, painted white, arranged in a squared off horseshoe around a dirt courtyard. Each building had a shallow-pitched roof of rusty corrugated metal, which overhung by several feet along the front and was supported by crooked tree branches. This provided shade for a cement slab that served as a veranda. Each building had a row of corrugated metal doors, which opened into separate houses. In Bojang's house there was a front room that served as his office. It contained his motorbike and a table piled high with papers and agricultural pamphlets. A room behind that had a bed with a comfortable straw mattress, a table with several family photographs neatly arranged on it, an old suitcase that served as a bureau, and a big earthenware jug that held drinking water. A door at the rear opened onto an area that was surrounded by a cement wall but open to the sky where one could bathe from a bucket and also use the toilet, a round hole in the cement floor. The entire area was very clean.

A few doors down from Bojang's house, a slender, middle-aged woman lived. He introduced her as "my mother." I was not sure if she was his real mother because Gambians have a way of adopting people in conversation. They say, "This is my sister," "This is my father," regardless of whether they are actually related. Directly across the courtyard "the old grandfather" lived. He was the owner of the compound and said to be over 100. He stayed indoors most of the time. I saw him only once as he shuffled off on a rare trip into the village; he stopped and greeted me very warmly. The other residents of the compound were young men and women, most of them teachers at the village school.

That evening, after dark, we all gathered in a circle in the courtyard. I was given a low, wooden bench to sit on. Most of the others squatted on their heels. Three large bowls of rice were placed on the sandy ground. One was topped with a whole fish, another with chunks of meat and gravy, the third with a sauce made from pounded groundnuts. We all ate directly from these common bowls. Bojang had given several of us spoons. The others ate in the Gambian tradition with their fingers. Someone aimed a weak flashlight beam in the general direction of the bowls so that we could see what we were eating.

A three-quarter-full moon was rising in the sky, and there were brilliant stars. Salikenni is beautiful in moonlight. The rusty, ragged fences are softened until you see only their function, which is to create privacy, to define a home. The sand lanes and courtyards, scorching by day, become silver pathways. A cool breeze carried the pleasing smell of charcoal fires and the sounds of distant voices and laughter.

"Eat," said Bojang.

"I am eating," I replied. "It's delicious."

"But you're not eating enough." With his own spoon, he deftly separated a choice piece of fish from the bone and pushed it to my side of the bowl. This is a common courtesy in a Gambian meal: The host or hostess, using a spoon or fingers, separates the best pieces and flicks them to the side of the common bowl closest to the guest.

Soon I witnessed another Gambian custom. Bojang shouted: *"Naa simango!"* (The ng in *simango* is soft.) The phrase means "Come and eat dinner!" He had seen a neighbor walk past the entrance to the compound. The circle made room for the newcomer, a middle-aged man in jeans and T-shirt. He took a few bites, said, "Thank you," then was off on whatever had been his original errand. I learned that often there may be several such visitors during a Gambian meal.

After dinner, someone lit a candle, which flickered in the slight breeze, and some of the teachers, who lived in the compound, began playing a game called Ludo, moving pieces around a board according to repeated throws of a single die. They moved the pieces very quickly, banging them loudly onto the board, followed by roars of laughter from onlookers when a player suffered a reversal. Six or eight school children, boys and girls, arrived and found places to sit. One by one they handed exercise books to their respective teachers, who held them at an angle to catch the candlelight, marked them and, in soft voices, explained any errors. These were grade six students who had volunteered for extra work to prepare for an exam. The children stayed for a while, watching the board game, and then drifted away.

The conversation in the courtyard continued late into the night. I was asked many questions.

"Does everyone in America have a car?"

"At night in America do you have a moon?"

"Is it the same moon as ours?"

The teachers wanted to know how to get scholarships to study in America. Some of them asked questions about U.S. government and foreign policy that showed they had considerable knowledge of America, much more than most Americans have about Africa.

Meanwhile, a young man, sitting on the edge of the group, was brewing Chinese green tea, which is locally called *ataya*. This drink is so common in The Gambia that it seems part of the very society. It is almost always prepared by a boy or young man, although women are equally skilled. The brewer puts water and tea and a lot of sugar into a small metal teapot and heats it on top of a little charcoal stove. After an initial brewing he pours some of the tea into two little glasses and then pours the contents of the glasses back into the pot for more brewing. He repeats this cycle several times. He holds the pot high as he pours into the little glasses. An *ataya* maker's skill is measured by how high he can hold the pot and direct a stream into the glasses without spilling a drop. Finally, when the tea is very strong and very sweet, he pours two glasses with great ceremony and hands them to two senior people in the group. They drink it quickly, then hand the glasses back to the maker. He refills them and offers them to others, and then he pours a final serving of two more. *Ataya* is the perfect drink to accompany conversation because the brewing is fun to watch and takes a long time. It is also a way in which a young man can attach himself to an older patron. This relationship may not be a lasting one. In time, someone younger will become the brewer.

Throughout the evening, people kept dropping into Bojang's compound. They sat and talked for a while and then took their leave. Mama Jobi, wearing a colorful long African dress, said her rice crop that year was poor. A farmer known as Mr. John said his groundnut crop, not yet harvested, looked promising. Another visitor was Abdoulie Kinteh, then headmaster of the Salikenni school. He invited me to visit the school the next day.

———◆+✳+◆———

When I first saw the Salikenni village school in 1991, it was a depressing sight. It was only a primary school then, grades one through six, and was a cluster of dingy cement-block buildings with roofs of rusty corrugate, surrounding a sandy open space. The classrooms inside were appalling. The plaster on the walls was

A Salikenni classroom in the 1990s. The blackboard is painted directly onto the plaster wall.

yellowed and flaking away. The floors were crumbling cement, full of potholes. There was not enough furniture. The children were squeezed onto narrow benches and placed their papers on scarred tabletops. The windows and doors were nothing but rough openings. Goats had wandered in and out during the night, leaving the floor filthy. A caretaker made a feeble effort each morning to sweep the uneven floor. There were no maps or posters or teaching materials of any kind on the walls. Teachers explained that, first, they had hardly any and, second, since the buildings could not be locked, anything left there could be vandalized.

Kinteh, a young-looking man, although he said he had been teaching in rural Gambian schools for 18 years, told me that grade three had 14 math textbooks; it should have had 62. Grade four had 25 math books and 7 English books; it needed 39 of each. At the time—the fourth week of the fall term—the education ministry had sent no exercise books, no pens, pencils, chalk or paper. Kinteh needed 11 teachers; he had 7.

Kinteh said he had seen many changes during his nearly two decades of teaching. The biggest was in people's attitudes toward education. In the "old days," he said, teachers went into compounds and begged parents to send their children to school. They went from neighborhood to neighborhood with drummers drumming, as they tried to gather crowds and make their pitch for education. Many parents in those days did not think education was necessary for farming. Many also felt that schooling was inappropriate for girls and that it might expose them to non-Muslim ideas. It was not needed for women's roles of raising children, cooking, cleaning and fetching water. But Kinteh said that, increasingly over the years, many parents were changing their minds about education and also about the size of families. The older generation had wanted many children so enough would survive to work the farms. Now, Kinteh said, many of the younger parents felt they wanted smaller families so they could afford to educate all their children, and those children could then support them in their old age.

I heard the same thing from others during that trip to The Gambia. A farmer in another village told me, "I know the value of education. It is the only way we will be able to develop. Our young people have to know something." Foday Trawalleh, a farmer active in community development in Salikenni, said, "Even if a young person goes to school and finds that no jobs are available, he or she will benefit. That person could be a very good farmer. He could grow more crops."

The Salikenni school in 1991 seemed typical of many others I saw in different parts of The Gambia and in other countries in East and West Africa. When the colonial powers withdrew from Africa in the 1960s they left behind almost no public education. For the most part they had set up only a few schools to train elite Africans for the civil service. In 1960, as independence was just dawning in sub-Saharan Africa, only 35 percent of the region's children of primary school age were in school. Among children of secondary school age the enrollment rate was only 3 percent. At the college level it was one-tenth of a percent. As they gained independence, African countries quickly adopted the goal of universal public education. But they couldn't pay for it. Across the continent newly independent African countries opened thousands of schools, but they lacked the money to train teachers fast enough or provide sufficient books or even adequate buildings. Many classes met outdoors in the shade of trees. The pattern in The Gambia was the same. In 1970, five years after the country's independence, only 27 percent of Gambian children of primary school age had been enrolled in school.

Over the next few years I made several more trips to Salikenni, not on a reporting mission but just as a visitor. Inevitably I found myself financing small projects at the school. I had made friends with a carpenter named Solomon Gabidon, who lived in the coastal village of Bakau; I hired him to build some desks and benches for the school. He also built window frames with wire mesh and put them into the bare masonry window openings of some of the classrooms. This allowed the classrooms to be locked up securely when not in use, which in turn allowed teachers to put up posters that they had made themselves.

During one of these visits, the school asked me to finance the construction of a kitchen building for preparation of the daily lunch for students. A group of village women were cooking big kettles of rice for this meal over a wood fire outdoors, even during the season of heavy rains. They worked without pay but were allowed to take leftover rice home to their families. For a very small price a donkey cart and several boys with spades were dispatched to the bush to bring back several loads of sand. Someone else went to Farafenni, a medium-sized town up river, and bought bags of cement, which arrived on the roof of a passenger van. School children were recruited to carry buckets of water from a tap in the schoolyard. Several village men and a few teachers began mixing the sand, cement and water right on the ground. They poured the mixture into a metal mold and turned the mold over to deposit one cement block at a time on the ground. I tried inexpertly to help in this process. After some time dozens and dozens of cement blocks were spread in rows across the yard, drying in the sun. Then hired masons began building the walls. As I prepared to leave at the end of my visit the walls were up to roof level. The teachers said that when the building was finished they planned to put my name on it. I said I really didn't want to have my name on a building. At my urging they promised not to use my name, and they kept their promise. When I returned to the village a year later, the building was complete and freshly painted white with green trim around the windows. A hand-written sign over the door proclaimed: "Alison May's Kitchen."

On one of my early visits to the village I sat down with Yahya Kalleh and Masaneh Kulijara Fatajo, two elderly men who were oral historians. Kalleh is a big man, heavily whiskered, with a booming voice, who wears traditional African robes. For many years he was a teacher of the Koran at the village school. He told me he had been dismissed from that job, just short of fully paid retirement, for openly backing an opposition political party. He was the head of a large compound just off the market square, and he was the father of Momodou Kalleh, who, in 1996, became the first Gambian manager of SSF. We sat in the shade of a large tree in the courtyard of Yahya Kalleh's compound.

The two historians told me that seven hundred years ago a man named Walimang Dibba was traveling through this area of grasslands and woods with a large retinue of wives and relatives. He and his group stopped and set up camp. Dibba was from Ouagadougou, in what is now Burkina Faso. At about the same time, a holy man named Janneh Ceesay was traveling with a group of scholars of the Koran. They stopped and set up their own camp some distance away.

One day while walking in the woods, Dibba and Cessay met. They decided to merge their camps and jointly establish a village.

A silk cotton tree on the road to Mandori.

They named it Salikenni, which means a sandy place to pray. They agreed on a division of authority. Dibba became the *alikalu*, or chief, of the village. Ceesay became the imam, the religious leader. Ever since then, with one exception, all the *alikalus* of Salikenni have been Dibbas, and all the imams have been Ceesays. (The Dibba line of succession was interrupted in 2012, when the president of The Gambia kicked out the then-Chief Dibba and installed his own man with a different surname.)

When the original Dibba and Ceesay first met, the local historians said, the area was heavily forested, and the great river flowed with fresh water. Now there were only scattered areas of trees, and the river at Salikenni was brackish. Several elderly farmers have told me they remember when the river water could be used to cultivate rice. Over many decades decreasing rainfall reduced the volume of water flowing downstream, so that tidal water from the Atlantic reached farther and farther upstream. In recent years, to grow rice on rain-fed land near the river, the village has had to construct low, earthen dikes to keep the salty water out of the rice paddies. According to the elder Kalleh and Fatajo, there were elephants and lions and other large animals in the woods when the village was founded, and the people hunted them. Now there were only hare and other small animals. When the village was new, people lived in grass houses, which were prone to terrible fires.

One subject about which the two historians had little to say was slavery. Each said they knew of no one in Salikenni whose ancestor was taken into slavery. Yet histories of The Gambia on several very informative tourist websites make clear that, from the 1400s to the 1800s, the Gambia River was a port of call for slave ships. First these were Portuguese ships, and one theory as to the origin of the name Gambia is that it came from the Portuguese word *cambio*, meaning exchange or trade. In the 1600s and beyond, British ships dominated the slave trade.

In the early 1800s, Britain turned against slavery and tried to prevent slave ships from other nations from using the Gambia River. The original British settlement at Bathurst, now Banjul, was established as an outpost to control the river and to prevent ships of other nations from using it in the slave trade. But even after 1833, when the British Parliament abolished slavery throughout its empire, slave ships continued to visit the Gambia River for several decades, according to these histories. All these accounts agree that slavery existed in West Africa long before the Atlantic slave trade began bringing slaves to America, and that Africans themselves captured most of the slaves and handed them over to the ship masters. In his book *Roots*, Alex Haley tells the story of his ancestor, Kunte Kinte, who, in 1767, was captured into slavery from his village of Juffure on the river, about 30 miles downstream from Salikenni, and was taken to America. Part of The Gambia's tourist industry today seeks to attract black Americans to come and explore their own roots.

The Salikenni Scholarship Fund grew out of an early morning walk in the village in October of 1996. A leisurely stroll, in the cool air before the sun rose above the rooftops, was an almost daily habit for me during visits to the village. It was quiet at that hour. The old men had finished praying in the mosques. They gathered in small groups on the lanes to chat, and greeted me as I walked by. A few people were headed down the path that led to the river, hoping to buy fish directly from the fishermen. The school children had not yet emerged from their compounds in their uniforms. Women and girls with basins waited at the public taps for the solar-powered water system to start flowing.

As I made my way along a lane a tall girl appeared by my side and walked with me. She was silent for a while and seemed to struggle to put her thoughts into English. Finally, she asked timidly, "Can you pay my school fees?"

I later learned that her name was Fatoumata Trawalley. She had a narrow face. Her hair was neatly arranged in little rows with a small tuft at the back. She was then, I think, 17. She had finished primary school six years earlier but had not been in school since then.

Before that time the Salikenni school stopped after grade six. Parents who wanted their children to attend grade seven and beyond had to send them to a school in one of the larger rural towns or to the Kombos, the Banjul metropolitan area. That meant finding relatives or friends who would house and feed them. Many parents feared their children, especially those at grade seven and eight levels, would be subjected to bad influences in these distant places. Also, the fees charged by government schools rose sharply at grade seven level. Like most African countries, The Gambia was far from being able to afford free public education for all children. In the late 1990s primary school fees in The Gambia were fairly low, about five dollars a year for grade six at the exchange rates of those days. The typical fee for middle school at that time was about $75 a year, and for high school about $186 a year. The average annual income per person in the country at that time was about $300, no doubt lower in rural areas. For a family with many children, these fees were unaffordable, and as a result many children dropped out of school, particularly after grade six.

In the fall of 1996 the government announced it would create a middle school in Salikenni for grades seven through nine. That opened an opportunity for Fatoumata—if someone would pay her fees. The middle school opened that fall in the primary classrooms after hours, then moved to the village youth center. (Several years later the government built new buildings for the middle school at the primary school site.)

I discussed Fatoumata's request with Momodou Kalleh, then deputy head of the Salikenni school and son of Yahya Kalleh, one of the two local historians who had told me about the origins of the village. I had worked with Momodou on the kitchen building and other projects at the school. He was 35 at the time, a man of medium height with a quiet manner. He smiled often, revealing a missing front tooth. Momodou had grown up in the family compound and attended the Salikenni primary school. His father had sent him to middle and high school in other towns. His first job had been as an uncertified teacher in a rural school in 1979. He had earned very little money and sent most of it home. He outfitted himself in used clothing. He had taken the exam to attend Gambia College to become certified, and had passed it three times but each time was rejected after an interview. He said hundreds of applicants would take the exam for only 45 openings. On the fourth try he passed both the exam and the interview. He attended the college, at government expense, for three years and earned a primary teaching certificate. He taught in several rural schools and then was posted in Salikenni.

Early in his teaching career Momodou fell in love. But his father said the young woman was from the wrong tribe and refused to permit the marriage. Momodou met another young woman, and the same thing happened again. Then, one day, while teaching in a rural village, he received a note from his father saying: "I have selected a wife for you. She is waiting in Salikenni." Her name was Binta. "I had never met the lady," Momodou told me. But he went ahead with the marriage, and it turned out to be a good and lasting one.

Muslim tradition allows a man to have up to four wives if he can support them. Momodou took three more wives. He divorced one, leaving a total of three who lasted. Binta continued to live in the senior Kalleh's compound with a growing number of children. Ndey lived in a compound in another part of the village. During visits to the village I often stayed in the house next to hers. Yamundow, the third wife, lived in the nearby town of Kerewan.

When I told Momodou about Fatoumata's request, his first suggestion was that her younger brother, Ebrima, might be a better candidate for education. He was not in school either, but he was bright and closer to the normal age for grade seven. Momodou went on to explain that the problem was much bigger than this brother and sister; many other Salikenni youngsters were unable to go beyond grade six because their families could not afford the fees. And, indeed, during that 1996 visit several other children approached me with the same request.

Over several evenings, sitting long after dark in the courtyard of Ndey's compound, slapping mosquitoes, Momodou and I developed the idea of a scholarship fund to meet this need. Momodou would select the students and I would raise the money to pay their fees.

He would manage the program locally as a volunteer. We reached agreement, and I returned to the United States. Alison and I, with legal help from our son-in-law, Henry Hart, applied for 501(c)3 status so that donations to the program would be tax exempt. The Internal Revenue Service quickly granted it. We announced the program in a newsletter that we sent by mail to people we knew, soliciting contributions.

Our first scholarship class that year had 31 students. Some were already in middle schools or higher in other parts of the country. Their parents needed help to keep up with the school fees. Others were attending the new Salikenni middle school. The school year had already begun when the middle school opened. Many of the potentially best students were already attending schools elsewhere. To fill the new grade seven class in Salikenni, teachers went around the village recruiting any candidates they could find. Many of these were dropouts who had been out of school for years. Our first group of scholarship students contained many such dropouts. In retrospect, we should have realized that educating them would be a challenge.

Fatoumata and her brother, Ebrima, were both included in that first group. Neither went very far in their education. Fatoumata made it only as far as grade nine. In the spring of that year she was supposed to take the exam that determines eligibility for high school, but she never gave Momodou the results. Perhaps she failed the exam; perhaps she never actually took it. The following school year, Momodou and I agreed to drop her. Ebrima failed his grade nine exam. We offered to pay for him to repeat that grade. Instead, his family put him into grade ten in Banjul Academy, a private high school in Banjul. I was very familiar with that school.

Several years earlier I had briefly sponsored a student there from a different part of the country. The school was a tuition mill. It would accept any student for whom a parent or a sponsor would pay. It provided little education. Its students often had no teachers and no books. We declined to pay for Ebrima to go there, and I did not hear anything further about him. Eventually, the government forced Banjul Academy to close.

A decade after we started the program, during another of my visits in Salikenni, Fatoumata came to see me. She said she wanted to thank me. For several years she had held a paid job with a Gambian nonprofit group teaching village women to read and write in Mandinka. That program had recently ended, and she was now working full-time, teaching in a nursery school that was sponsored by a group from Germany and was located in the Salikenni youth center.

"It was because of the little education that you gave me that I was able to have these jobs," Fatoumata said.

CHAPTER 4

Becoming a Family

ON A HUMID DAY in August 1999, in the middle of the West African rainy season, Ebrima M. Fatty took me to see his farm.

Ebrima was 17 then, an outgoing boy, small for his age. He came from a compound of mud-brick houses in Ba Santo, an especially poor neighborhood in Salikenni. His father, Mohammad Fatty, was a farmer who now spent much of each year in Banjul, working as a petty trader, selling used clothing and other goods in the city's streets.

Ebrima M. Fatty (left) weeding with his brother, Abdoulie, in 1990.

Ebrima is one of the success stories from the early years of SSF, when Momodou Kalleh was coordinator. Ebrima joined the program in the fall of 1998, when he was starting grade nine at the village school. His father had paid his school fees until then but could no longer do so. A teacher called our attention to Ebrima, saying he was a good student and that it would be a shame if he had to drop out of school.

Men weeding groundnuts.

Agriculture in Salikenni traditionally is divided by gender. The men grow groundnuts, which are the principal cash crop and the country's main export. The men grow other cash crops, too, including coos, a grain related to millet, and sometimes corn. The women grow rice, the staple food. The growing season for all of these crops is the rainy season, which normally begins in June and lasts through October. During the rest of the year, it virtually never rains, and the plain outside the village turns brown as far as the

Women harvesting rice.

eye can see. During those months the only substantial agriculture is in community vegetable gardens operated by the women and irrigated from hand-dug wells. The men have relatively little to do during the dry months except talk politics.

On a typical workday in the growing season there is a mild early morning rush hour as men and boys head out of the village on sand roads into the countryside. Some walk, carrying hoes and cutlasses. A few ride bicycles. Most ride out on carts, their legs dangling over the sides. The carts are almost all alike, a wooden platform with wooden shafts, mounted on an old automobile axle with pneumatic tires. Most are pulled by donkeys, some by horses, and a few by lumbering bulls. The drivers are often young boys who stand up, holding a stick in the air, and shout, "*Acha! acha!*" to make the animals go faster. Smaller boys ride donkeys or horses bareback to deliver them to the men in the fields.

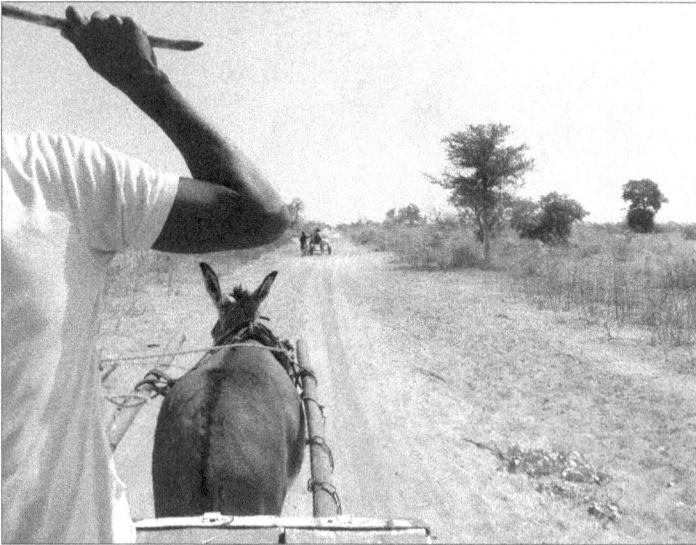

To make the donkey go the driver raises his stick and shouts "Acha!"

Agriculture is so central in the life of the village that I wanted to find out more about it. Ebrima and I walked about 15 minutes through the green plain. It was a sunny day with small dark clouds racing across the sky. The Gambia seldom has continuous rain for very long. More often the rainy season takes the form of scattered showers and violent cloudbursts.

The farm plots are small—some maybe 20 by 50 yards. They are not marked or fenced. Their boundaries are known by "that tree" or "this bush."

We stopped at a smallish field filled with groundnut plants, ankle high with small leaves. "This is my farm," Ebrima said with a big smile. He said his father had given him complete responsibility over it for the current season.

His two younger brothers, Abdoulie and Baba, were already there. They had hitched their donkey to a plow, which would be used that day to weed the field. The plow had a wooden frame and long wooden handles with an iron wheel in front and a single iron blade that arced down to dig into the ground. The boys began weeding. Abdoulie walked beside the donkey, leading it between two rows of groundnuts. Ebrima walked behind, holding the handles. The plow blade pulled up the weeds between the rows. They went back and forth, row after row. Later the boys would have to go over the field again with small hand hoes, pulling up the weeds between the individual plants in each row.

Ebrima told me that during the previous rainy season, his father had not farmed at all. He had stayed in the Banjul area to try his hand at business. That year the boys had sowed and weeded and harvested a groundnut field themselves. They had harvested only one "donkey" of groundnuts. A "donkey" is two big bags, the amount that will fit on the animal's back. At the beginning of this year's growing season the boys went to the local farm co-op hoping

Bringing home the crop.

to borrow fertilizer against their future crop. They were told that one donkey the previous year did not qualify them for even one bag of fertilizer. So the current crop had not been fertilized. Despite this, the groundnut plants seemed green and strong, possibly because this particular field had been fallow the previous year. During the next season it would be planted in coos.

This kind of agriculture hasn't changed much in a century in The Gambia. Some call it subsistence farming, but I think of it as less-than-subsistence farming. I know of very few Salikenni families who actually earn their entire living from their farms. Almost all of them depend on a relative or two who have gone to the urban area, or to Europe or America, and have found some kind of work and from time to time send money home.

August is the month when the problems of this type of agriculture come to a head. In a good year the rice grown by the women to feed their families may last only four to six months. Then families start buying rice, using cash from their previous groundnut harvest. But by August this cash is gone. So families start borrowing rice from local shops, promising to pay after their next groundnut harvest. When that harvest finally comes, much of the earnings go to pay the previous debt.

August and September have been called the hungry season in West Africa because many families then must start reducing their daily diets. They switch from rice to coos. Many begin skipping meals. A compound will serve two meals a day instead of three. The local health clinic begins to see an increase in the number of malnourished children. This also is the time of year when people must work the hardest. And it is the height of the mosquito season, when malaria is most dangerous.

As Ebrima and I looked out across the plain, we could see in the distance other farmers working their fields with donkeys, horses, bulls, or just by hand. It was quiet on the plain. Occasionally from far away we could hear a muted shout: "*Acha!*" One sound we did not hear was that of an internal combustion engine—not a tractor, not even a truck on a distant highway.

"We Gambian farmers are working with our energy," Ebrima told me that day. "We use our bodies to work. Our parents borrow rice. When they sell their groundnuts there is no profit left. It is because of lack of machines."

We walked back to the village in a gentle shower with the sun still shining. Ebrima told me his ambition was to go to a university, maybe in America, and study agriculture.

"I want to learn the machines," he said, "to do something about Gambian agriculture."

A month after this walk to his farm, Ebrima started high school at Gambia Senior Secondary School in Banjul under our scholarship. His passion for agriculture continued, but he also became fascinated with literature, and he told us that someday he would like to write a novel. "History is the fallacy of generalization," he once told me. "But literature is true. You see it so clearly." In the spring of 2002 Ebrima became the first in his family to graduate from high school.

Ebrima wanted to go to the University of The Gambia to study agriculture and literature, but his high school results did not meet the entry criteria. His second choice was Gambia College, run by the government, which had a tuition-free program to upgrade the skills of agricultural extension workers. A college admissions person told him that all the openings in that program had been filled by existing extension workers, but he could attend the class as a tuition-paying student. We agreed to pay for the three-year course. Ebrima received a Certificate in General Agriculture in 2005; that should have led to a job as an extension worker. But the government told him he was ineligible because he had been a student from outside, not previously in the extension service.

So we paid for Ebrima to go back to Gambia College, this time to be trained as a teacher of agriculture. In 2008 he received a Higher Diploma in Agriculture, certifying him to teach in secondary schools.

In 2009 he was hired to teach agricultural science at the Latrikunda Upper Basic School, a big middle school in the suburbs of Banjul. He also was the master of the school garden, which he used to demonstrate the practical side of the courses he taught.

Ebrima M. Fatty, graduate of Gambia College, now a teacher.

While continuing to teach, Ebrima began studies at the university for a bachelor's degree in agriculture. We agreed to pay that tuition. (His studies have since been delayed a number of times because of conflicts with his teaching.)

During the 2011 growing season, a severe drought hit most of the Sahel, the region that stretches across Africa just under the Sahara. We knew that The Gambia, which is part of the region, was seriously affected, but we had few details. In 2012 Ebrima, on his own initiative, volunteered to carry out an ambitious project to learn more. He went to Salikenni and interviewed 100 farming households. Ebrima found that 54 percent of households had cut back to two meals a day from three, usually skipping breakfast; 46 percent said they had not cut meals but were now leaving "the other expenses to God," including school fees; and 97 percent said they had gone deeper into debt. Ebrima's written report included a series of recommendations—more research on the effects of water deficit on crops, efforts to increase yields per hectare, better weather forecasting, greater use of drought-resistant varieties of crops, irrigation and drainage methods, and better coordination between research and extension services.

"Agriculture is developing slowly in The Gambia," Ebrima said in a recent email to Alison and me. Referring to that day long ago when he showed me his farm, he added, "At the local level . . . it has not developed much. My father and my younger brothers in Salikenni are still using the same crude tools."

He said that only a few farms in the country have advanced from the subsistence level to larger-scale production. He listed a handful of fairly large commercial farms, one of which is owned by the president of the country. There is now a commercial tractor based in Salikenni, but few farmers can afford to hire it to plow their fields. In order to develop further, Ebrima said, farmers need to be better educated, more teachers, researchers and extension workers need to be trained, and mechanized farming must become more available.

Ebrima has become an active participant in the student-led management of SSF. Though not a member of the board, he attends planning meetings, gives advice, and is always willing to take on a specific chore. He recently told me in an email that his father was living once more in Salikenni. His mother was living in the rural town of Kerewan. Both of his younger brothers whom I had met have long since dropped out of school for financial reasons: Abdoulie was "doing petty trade" with an uncle in Banjul; Baba was working as a mason.

———————

Jainaba Dibba is another early success story. She was in the first group of SSF students when the program started in 1996. She was then in grade seven. In August 1999, a few days after visiting Ebrima's farm, I went to Jainaba's family compound in Salikenni, hoping to learn about the women's side of village agriculture.

I went on a Wednesday because, by tradition, Salikenni men and women don't go to the fields that day. I found Jainaba hanging up laundry.

She was dressed in work clothes, a simple long skirt with a blue design and a maroon blouse. She had just returned from the public water tap in her neighborhood with a basin of water on her head. So it was not exactly a day of rest.

At that time, Jainaba had finished grade nine at the village school. She was spending the summer at home before starting the next step in her education, high school in the Banjul metropolitan area.

A few weeks earlier she had attended the annual Gambia Student Union Congress in Banjul. That honor came because she had received the highest marks among girls in her Salikenni class. Gambian schools throughout the country send their top boy and girl to this congress to discuss national affairs. The top boy from Salikenni that year was Ebrima Fatty.

Jainaba told me that her father, Alhaji Abdoulie Dibba, the head of the family compound, who was in his 90s, was critically ill. He died the following day. He was a colorful figure, known far beyond the village. Though a native of Salikenni, he had lived for a number of years in Senegal and had found employment there. With the money he earned he had performed many acts of charity in the village.

Jainaba was Alhaji Abdoulie Dibba's youngest child; her mother had died many years earlier. Jainaba had been raised by her stepmother, Sarinbanding Trawalley. I could see that this family had a high regard for education. A sister, Awa, was about to finish high school in Banjul. She was married to a Gambian man who currently lived in the United States; he was paying for her education. Another sister, Oumie, and a brother, Adama, had completed high school, paid for by their father.

Another brother, Lamin Dibba, had also finished high school and then had decided to return to his village and to the land. He was a favorite of a series of U.S. Peace Corps volunteers who served in the village, usually in two-year postings. They found in Lamin someone they could work with and someone eager to test new kinds of agriculture. With their help over several years Lamin developed a large farm and orchard outside the village. He harvested and sold cashew nuts, guavas, oranges, mangos, bananas and other fruits. He also sold seedlings of those species. He raised bees and sold the honey and experimented with "live" fences woven of living vines, an ancient system being promoted by the Peace Corps and other groups. If built properly, the fences grow thick and strong and keep goats and other animals out of the farm plots. They are cheaper than barbed wire and longer-lasting than fences woven of dead reeds. But they require a lot of care, and have not become very popular in Salikenni.

After their father died, Lamin became Jainaba's guardian. He encouraged her education. He once told me he had rejected a suitor for Jainaba's hand because he wanted her to finish her education before marriage.

Jainaba's typical day, during those summer holidays, started at dawn or a little before. She would build a wood fire and cook breakfast for the compound. Breakfast was often rice porridge. After breakfast there were other chores that are done almost exclusively by women and girls—fetching water from the public taps and pounding grain. Later, she would rebuild the wood fire and start cooking lunch. If chicken was available to put on top of the day's rice, she would kill, pluck and cook it. If the topping would be fish, she would start by cleaning it.

During the growing season, long before lunch was served in the compound, Jainaba would put a little rice in a small basin and carry it on her head out to the rice fields, accompanied by her stepmother. They would not return until the sun was setting. Then there would be time to bathe, put on clean clothes and have dinner, prepared by other women in the compound.

During the dry season, Jainaba and her stepmother walked to a women's community garden outside the village. The garden, still in use today, is a large, fenced area with dozens of very small individual plots. Women grow lettuce, okra, bitter tomatoes and other vegetables, each in her own plot. They irrigate from open wells. They drop buckets down on ropes, sometimes 20 or more yards deep, and pull them up, hand over hand, without the benefit of any type of pulley or winch. They then carry the water to their individual plots and pour it onto one small section. The sandy soil absorbs the water instantly; in a few seconds the spot no longer looks wet. Then they go back to the well and fill another bucket. The women use some of the vegetables to feed their families. Many take some of the produce to sell at a weekly *lumo*, or market, in the village of Ker Pate, more than an hour away by horse cart. When she was in school in Salikenni during the dry season, Jainaba regularly went to the vegetable garden with her stepmother.

The day after my visit to her compound, Jainaba had planned to take me with her to see her rice field. Her father's death precluded this, but another of our scholarship students, named Fatoumata Fatty (not the same Fatoumata Fatty who later served on the SSF board), then in grade nine, agreed to take me to her own field a few days later.

"What time would you like to leave?" she asked.

Without thinking, I suggested 9 a.m., and she agreed. She came to collect me at the precise hour. She carried a blue plastic bucket, which she said contained her work clothes. But she had no food or water with her. I learned later that the women in her compound never went to the rice fields that early. The morning cooking had not been completed; she had come without having eaten breakfast and without bringing anything for her lunch.

Men on carts follow roads to their farms; the women walk to their rice fields on narrow footpaths. Fatoumata and I followed one of these down a very gradual slope from the village until we came to an area of dozens of rectangular rice paddies. Then we walked on top of an earthen dike, 1 or 2 feet wide and a foot high, with paddies full of water on each side. We took a meandering route across the tops of several dikes until we came to a small paddy, which Fatoumata said was hers. It was perhaps 20 feet square, reasonably thick with young rice plants about 8 inches tall. The soil was moist but there was no standing water as there was in several of the paddies we had passed. Fatoumata explained that those had clay soil while hers had sandy soil. She said both would produce rice.

She kicked off her sandals and began to weed, bending low with legs straight, pulling out the weeds and grass with her fingers, root by root.

I learned that this rice, and all that was growing in the nearby fields, had been sown in "broadcast" style, with the seeds having been scattered by hand rather than planted in rows. Fatoumata explained that because of this you could not weed with a hoe. The rice plants were too close together in a random pattern. Sometimes, when the soil was too dry she could not pull the grass out with her fingers. Then she used a small knife to pry each blade of grass out.

Jainaba told me later that she had learned in agricultural science class that rice should be sown in rows for efficient weeding. But she said none of the Salikenni women did so, including her stepmother.

I offered to help Fatoumata weed, but I soon found that my big shoes were not suited to the task. It was almost impossible to avoid stepping on the little shoots of rice that I was supposed to help protect.

There were no other women in the paddies nearby when Fatoumata and I began. But as we worked, more and more came. There were young girls, mothers with babies on their backs and old women who walked slowly, clearly in pain. They wore long skirts and loose blouses. By 11:30 a.m. in every direction I looked there was a woman bending over in the fields.

Fatoumata and I returned to the village shortly after noon. Normally, she would have kept working until dusk.

Later during that same visit to The Gambia, around 6:30 one evening, I was sitting on a small *banteba* made of sticks beside a road at the edge of the village, chatting with a teacher named Abdoulie Jarju. Most of the men and boys had long since returned with their carts from the groundnut fields. As we talked, a procession of young children came down the road toward the village, leading animals—goats, donkeys and a few cows. These had been staked out in the grass to graze during the day and the children had been sent to fetch them home for the night.

At that hour the women were beginning to return from the rice fields. They came at first one or two at a time, carrying their basins or bundles on their heads. They came from the west, where a brilliant red sunset lit the clouds and sky; they were silhouetted against it. As my watch moved to 7 p.m. and then 7:30 p.m. and the light faded, they came in larger numbers, one or two dozen at a time. Many walked single file, a few side-by-side, but with little conversation. Their sandals flip-flopped on the dirt road. As each group of women passed, Jarju would say to them quietly, "*I nimbara.*" This is a Mandinka expression (pronounced EE nim-BAR-ah) that literally means "you and work." But it implies praise for work, very like our expression "keep up the good work." As it grew quite dark the women still passed, and Jarju said quietly to each passing group, "*I nimbara.*" It was as though the secretaries of New York City were streaming out of the subway on their way home after a long day, and someone was there saying, "Good work. Keep up the good work."

In the years that followed that visit, Jainaba went on to become one of our most successful students. She finished grade nine at the top of her class. She graduated from high school in the metropolitan area in 2002. On her own initiative, she applied and was admitted to the free, three-year teacher-training program at Gambia College. She received a Higher Teaching Certificate from the college in 2005, which qualified her to teach in middle and high schools.

Jainaba taught for a year in a small village school. Since 2006 she has taught social and environmental studies at Brikama Upper Basic School on the outskirts of the Banjul metropolitan area. It is a big school and includes grades seven through nine.

In 2006 Jainaba married Lamin Samateh, a building contractor. They live in Brikama with their children. Jainaba also has become a participant in the student management of SSF, though not an actual board member. She has attended many meetings and serves as a role model for younger girls in the program.

———•◦•◦•———

Along with the successes in the early program, we also had our share of failures. A report to contributors dated March 1998 contained a picture of Kaddy Ndow, an apparently confident young woman in a white blouse, with a broad smile that revealed very even, white teeth. She was among the first students in the program. Her mother was one of the cooks who prepared lunch for the children at the school. Kaddy's father was dead; two of her uncles helped support the family. Kaddy had completed the Salikenni primary school in 1992. In those days graduates of grade six took a nationwide exam that determined eligibility for middle school.

(That exam is no longer given.) Kaddy did so well on the exam that the authorities said she could go directly into high school. She entered Muslim Senior Secondary School in Banjul. But three months later, when her family could not pay her fee, she was sent home. She was out of school until the fall of 1996 when she was admitted to our program in grade seven in Salikenni, at the age of 18. Our records are a bit unclear, but it seems that the school soon jumped her ahead a year, possibly because of her age. In the spring of 1998 she was in grade nine in Salikenni and took the nationwide exam to qualify for high school. She failed it.

In November of that year, having heard nothing further about her, Momodou and I tracked her down in a squalid house in Banjul, occupied by someone in her extended family. In contrast to the sparkling girl in the photo the previous March, she was uncommunicative and obviously depressed. She said she was looking for a school that would accept her.

We held an emotional meeting with Kaddy and several of her relatives. An older brother, Abubakarr, did most of the talking for the family. We urged that Kaddy repeat grade nine, but Abubakarr insisted that she was a "mature" girl and should be in grade ten. We said she was not prepared for grade ten. Kaddy sat silently during the meeting. It was clear that she had no role in deciding her future. We left the family to make its decision. We returned to Salikenni and met with Kaddy's mother. She said she understood our position. She very much wanted Kaddy to complete her education.

I heard nothing further until I was back in the United States. Momodou told me by phone that Kaddy's family had enrolled her in the tuition mill, Banjul Academy. We declined to pay for Kaddy there. I don't know how long she attended the school. I heard much later that she had married a man who sold clothing at the market in Serrekunda in the suburbs of Banjul.

———

Baba Trawalley was another member of the first class in 1996. He told us he was born in 1966, which would have made him 30 at the time. Whether or not that was exactly correct, he was a man of medium height with a thin mustache, a beard and a deep voice. He grew up in Salikenni, the son of a blacksmith who also was a goldsmith. He started primary school very late and finished grade six in 1986, at the age of 20. For the next ten years he had no schooling. He worked with his father, farming and perfecting his skills in the smith's trade.

Momodou believed that Baba had a strong desire for education. "He was all the time going 'round with students, reading their books, trying to learn English," Momodou told me during one of my visits. "If I asked him a question he would reply in English. I knew he wanted to be in school. I asked him about it one day, and he jumped at the chance."

I didn't have an opportunity to meet Baba until 1998. He invited me to his compound, a group of mud-brick buildings in Salikenni, where a ceremony was in progress to name a two-week-old baby girl, the daughter of Baba's older brother, Lamin. The men, dressed in their best kaftans, were distributing kola nuts among themselves. The women were cooking. The family had spent a lot of money buying bottles of soft drinks, which were in tubs of ice water. Tradition calls for a naming ceremony to be held seven days after a child is born. The name is secret until it is announced at the ceremony. There were many long speeches in Mandinka. A goat had been slaughtered and cooked. The women brought out basins of rice. Baba gave me a letter to deliver to an American couple who had contributed financially to SSF and who had exchanged letters with him for some time. He also asked me to deliver to them two silver "love rings" with jet black stones, which he had made for them. When I asked admiringly what the stones were, he said they came from the plastic cover of an audio cassette.

A short time later, Baba failed his grade nine exam. Armed with a letter of recommendation from a crooked principal, he talked his way into a provincial high school. He dropped out during the third term of grade ten, telling Momodou that he was suffering from an eye problem. We suspected that he was simply over his head in high school.

—◆•◈•◆—

These two cases illustrate some shortcomings of the early SSF program: The selection of students was solely up to Momodou. We were not at all sophisticated in judging the academic ability of students we admitted. We would give anyone a chance and see what would happen. We had little contact with parents and no plan to involve them in the education of their children. Nor were we closely monitoring or mentoring our students. We paid their fees and hoped for the best, but the students were on their own.

To make matters worse, during the first years of our program, the Salikenni school was in chaos. It had a new principal, who arrived amid rumors that he had gotten into trouble for financial mismanagement at a previous school. He spent little time at the

Salikenni school. Villagers said he invited his students to parties where alcohol and marijuana were used—both forbidden by Muslim tradition. In the classrooms there was a serious breakdown of discipline. Many of the teachers were Nigerians. They didn't speak Mandinka. Their English pronunciation was different. The students taunted them; the teachers gave up on the students. The principal eventually was audited by the Ministry of Education and was unable to account for large amounts of school fees that had been paid. His punishment was one we have seen a number of times: He was transferred to another school. After that there was a fairly rapid turnover of principals in Salikenni. Several of these made serious efforts to create a better learning environment. The best ones, for one reason or another, didn't stay long enough to have a real impact.

Momodou Kalleh, however, was always looking for young people whom the education system had bypassed but in whom he saw talent. One of these was a strong, husky boy named Lamin Mai Trawalley, who often hung around the Kalleh compound, listening to the adults talk and brewing green tea for them. In 1997, at the age of 14, Lamin had never been to school. He spoke no English. But Momodou recognized his intellectual potential, and he asked if we would agree to give Lamin an education. We did.

But to attend the Salikenni school, Lamin had to first learn English. Momodou started him out in grade two. In his crisp uniform—blue shorts and white shirt—Lamin towered over his classmates. He was friendly to everyone. He learned English quickly. He was rapidly promoted and finished primary school in two years.

In grades seven through nine in Salikenni, Lamin was a reasonably good student. One thing that impressed us was that he applied what he learned in agricultural science class to the farm that he worked with his father. He experimented with mixed cropping—sowing groundnuts and beans together. Unable to afford fertilizer, he begged manure from neighbors who owned animals. During the dry season he tried growing vegetables on a tiny plot of his own, irrigating it with buckets of water drawn from a nearby well. Insects ate up most of his crop. Lamin acquired a small yellow dog that he named Lemon, who would follow him out to the garden.

One day during the dry season, Lamin and I stood at the top of a low hill outside Salikenni, looking down a long, gradual slope covered by useless brown grass and a few shrubs. "If I were president there would be irrigation here," Lamin said. He described a system pictured in one of his books: a borehole, a pump, solar panels and plastic tubing. The land stretching before us would be green. Agriculture would become truly profitable. Instead of so many young people leaving for the cities, people would be coming back to the land.

Lamin's teachers were sure he would do well on the grade nine exam. But he missed the government cutoff mark by two points. That ruled out the major high schools in the Banjul area. In the fall of 2002 he began grade ten in Farafenni, a dusty town about 25 miles upriver from Salikenni. He lived in a compound there. But the owner's wife made him feel unwelcome and gave him little food. After one term, Momodou transferred him to another rural high school at Njaba Kunda. That school was just getting started, and Lamin felt it was bringing in unruly and even violent students. He pleaded to be transferred to a Kombos school. Two high schools turned him down but, in 2003, Kotu Senior Secondary in the Banjul suburbs accepted him in grade eleven. In hindsight, he was not ready for the Kombos.

Lamin by this time had developed an interest in the world. He had a small radio and listened daily to the BBC news. He knew the names of African leaders and American presidential candidates. His spoken English was becoming quite good. He discovered literature. He read *Robinson Crusoe* and *The Old Man and the Sea* and asked for more. But his schoolwork went very badly. His grade eleven year ended in failure.

Lamin attributed this to his living conditions in the urban area. For a time he lived with a family of tailors and slept on a mat on the floor of their shop after it closed each night. Later he found a better place to live. But he said he fell in with a group of boys who were not in school, and he spent more time with them than he did studying.

Kotu allowed him to repeat grade eleven, but that school year, 2004–05, went no better. This was the same year that we hired a new manager to replace Momodou Kalleh, as described later in this chapter. Lamin was deeply upset by this change. He was very loyal to Momodou and urged us to reinstate him. We learned that Lamin was seldom attending school. It took a lot of coaxing to get him even to come to the compound of the new manager for a talk. When he finally did come he seemed depressed and troubled. He said he still wanted an education and a career in Gambian agriculture. But, he added, "When I start to study, someone makes me angry, and I cannot understand."

He said he wanted to drop out of school and study on his own. He wanted us to give him private tutoring. We invited him to attend weekend tutoring classes that we had begun in math and English. Lamin went off to think this over. He never returned for the weekend classes.

Later that same month, I ran into Lamin's father, Ebrima Trawalley, in Salikenni. Through a translator, the old man told me he had no idea his son was failing in school. Momodou Kalleh had never mentioned anything like this to him. Lamin's experience taught us just how important communication with parents is in a program such as ours.

I didn't see Lamin again until 2011. I was in Salikenni and heard that he was in the village, and I sent a message asking him to come to the compound where I was staying. He showed up at 8:00 in the evening, saying he had come at night so no one would see him. When I asked why he did not want to be seen, he only referred to the "changes" a year earlier, indicating that the replacement of Momodou was still troubling him.

I asked Lamin what he was doing at the time. He replied that he would have to start at the beginning. He said that after he left Kotu, without completing grade eleven, the Salikenni school hired him to be a volunteer teacher because it was very short-handed. He worked there for three weeks. Then he got a letter from Momodou, offering the same job at a village called Minta Kunda, where Momodou had been appointed principal. Lamin went to work for Momodou, who later encouraged him to take the entrance examination for Gambia College's teacher-training program. Lamin took the exam and passed. He attended the three-year course and was certified as a primary school teacher. He was told to report to a village called

Dibba Kunda, upriver. But he read in a newspaper that there was a food shortage there, and he refused the assignment. He was given a new assignment farther upriver. But he said he fell ill for a month, and when he finally reported for work, the school no longer needed him. His final posting was even farther upriver. "Life there is terrible," he said. The people of the village were primarily Wolof and Fula, he said, and they were "really provincial." He was assigned to live in a hut with a roof of palm leaves. "I could see the moon through the roof," he recalled. The door was made of sticks tied together. It could not be locked. One day while he was teaching, some money was stolen from his hut.

Lamin had recently married a young woman from Kerewan named Salimata, a high school graduate. Before the ceremony she made him promise he would take only one wife. At the time of this conversation, she was living in the suburbs of Banjul and was taking a computer course at a local business and trade college.

I ran into Lamin again in April 2013 during a visit to Salikenni. He had given up teaching. He said it didn't pay enough. He said he had a one-year job in Salikenni, working for a Taiwan-based organization that was trying to introduce a new kind of quicker-maturing rice into The Gambia. He was hoping to be hired by another organization that was trying to expand Salikenni's rice-growing area by building a series of dikes to keep the salty river water out of the rain-fed rice fields. His wife and son were living in Kerewan.

Lamin said he wanted to thank me for the partial education we gave him. "Otherwise," he said, "I would be a subsistence farmer."

Momodou Kalleh was the manager of SSF for almost nine years, from 1996 until the middle of the 2004–05 school year. During that period the program grew from an initial 31 students to 47. Of these, 25 were in grades seven through nine, mostly in Salikenni; 17 were in high schools, mainly in the urban area; and five were in urban, post-secondary technical and business schools.

Our annual spending grew from $3,200 the first year to $14,370 during 2003–04. There were several reasons for that increase. We had more students, and more were at levels of higher tuition. We had started tutoring programs both in Salikenni and the metropolitan area. There was a one-time cost of shipping 1,000 books across the ocean for the school library. And we had begun paying Momodou, who had started as a volunteer, a stipend of about $300 a year. Our administrative costs stood at 10 percent of total spending.

At the end of 2004–05 Alison and I went through our records going back to 1996 to determine the overall success rate for the program. Our research showed that, in addition to 47 students then in the program, 61 had entered over the years and left for one reason or another. Of those 61, 29 (48 percent) had finished high school, including ten who had gone on to some kind of higher education, either at our expense or the government's. But 32 students (52 percent) had dropped out or had been dropped by us, without finishing high school.

The above figures do not include about eight students whom Momodou had listed as current scholarship recipients but whose identities were a mystery to us. On each visit to The Gambia I had tried to interview as many of our students as possible. But there were always some who were unavailable for one plausible reason or another. Some students I had never met, because they had been unavailable year after year. Before my trip in the fall of 2001, I told Momodou I wanted to meet these elusive students. When I arrived in the country he produced all of them over a period of days. But there was one puzzling thing. In each case, the student had changed both his name and his school. For example, Alagie Njie, whom Momodou's accounting had listed as receiving our scholarship aid since 1996 at the New Era junior and senior schools, had transferred that year to Gambia Senior Secondary School and had changed his name to Kajali Dibba. Momodou told me that Salikenni boys often took the name of an older person they admired as their own nickname. He said that when they reached high school the schools would tell them to switch back to their real names so they could graduate with the correct name. But the story did not add up. I later checked the records at Gambia Senior Secondary. They showed that Kijali Dibba did not transfer to that school in 2001, as Momodou claimed. He had been a student there since 1998. From this and other cases, Alison and I concluded that Momodou had long been skimming money out of SSF by listing phantom students in his accounts and was now trying to cover his tracks. But proving it would be difficult. I did not look forward to an emotional confrontation. It was easier to leave the issue unresolved, but to check our student lists more carefully in the future.

That left us with another unsettling puzzle. Why, even excluding these phantom students, had only slightly less than half of our students since 1996 made it through high school? We could identify a number of possible reasons:

- One was a dilemma inherent in the way we selected our students. We chose to focus on those in financial need. We didn't, particularly in the early years of the program, have a very sophisticated way of discovering which among the needy applicants showed academic promise. Various people, some American and some Gambian, told us we should automatically select the top scorers on the previous year's sixth-grade exam. But those were not necessarily the ones with the most financial need.
- Another factor was that we weren't doing enough to encourage and motivate our students to do their best. I made brief visits one or two times a year. But, in between, Momodou seemed to treat the students with a "sink or swim" approach.
- Even more important, we didn't do enough to get the parents involved in their child's education. We had several cases where a student was failing, like Lamin, but his parents had no idea that this was happening.
- On top of all of this we had, in those days, no real mechanism to give special encouragement and help to the girls in the program, who, with some notable exceptions, tended to fail and drop out at a higher rate than boys.

Possibly, over time, Momodou and we could have overcome these problems. But events not directly related to the SSF scholarship program brought his tenure to a sudden end.

Parallel to the scholarship program, Alison and I had for years been using our own money—not SSF funds—to finance a series of improvement projects at the school. These included plastering and painting some of the classrooms, hiring carpenters to repair or replace broken benches and desks, buying tools for a school vegetable garden, and fencing some school land to start an orchard of fruit trees. Most of these projects had little success. The vegetable garden failed for lack of watering. Only a handful of young trees survived in the orchard. One metropolitan area carpenter took our money to buy wood to make desks for the school but never produced them.

In 1998 Momodou and I created a local committee to manage these non-SSF projects at the school. It was called *Londi Kaffo*, which means education group. Its members were three village men, a village woman, Momodou and me. Momodou picked the village members, who were all farmers and all of whom had children in various schools, though none were SSF students.

One of *Londi Kaffo's* most expensive projects was designed to supplement the school's lunch program. The United Nations World Food Programme was supplying rice and tinned meat and vegetable oil to rural schools in The Gambia, including Salikenni. But Salikenni school officials said these supplies were not sufficient. They needed spices and occasional fresh vegetables and fish to make the meals palatable and more nourishing. For several years Alison and I financed these extras. But in late 2004 we were having second thoughts about it. The cost had risen to about $250 a month. We were becoming less sure about how the money was being used and whether it fulfilled a real need. We informed Momodou that we could not continue the lunch program.

In November 2004, we received a faxed message from Momodou and members of the *Londi Kaffo* committee. They proposed that Alison and I finance a breakfast program for first- and second-grade children at the school. The committee said that many young children were coming to school with no breakfast, and that teachers and parents alike agreed that a child cannot learn on an empty stomach. The proposed breakfast could consist of coos, pounded into a powder and mixed with water or milk. The message asked us to send 20,000 dalasis (at the time, $640) that would buy 40 bags of coos, which would last all year. Since coos was relatively cheap at the time, the message noted, it made sense to buy a large quantity and store it. The request bore the names not only of *Londi Kaffo* members but also of a number of prominent people in the village who had been active in supporting the school. Since it seemed to come from a broad group, we sent the money.

Over the next few months we received reports from Momodou that the breakfast program was running smoothly. But I was also in direct touch by telephone with the principal of the school, Bai Jawara, and several of his teachers. They told me there was no breakfast program. They also said that, during the earlier lunch program, they had never received from *Londi Kaffo* amounts of food anywhere near what would be in line with the amount of money we had been sending.

Momodou claimed that school officials were lying in order to discredit *Londi Kaffo* in the hopes that we would send our assistance directly to the school so they could steal it. He insisted that breakfast was being served every morning. Over a period of several weeks, I made numerous international phone calls to each camp. Each insisted the other was lying. Alison and I were thousands of miles away, and at first we did not know whom to believe. It wasn't feasible to rush over to The Gambia and dive into a heated local controversy.

Gradually, it became clear that Momodou and *Londi Kaffo* were deceiving us. In mid-December 2004, I learned for the first time that Momodou was no longer deputy at the Salikenni school. He had been transferred in September to another school in the region, but had not informed us. So, for months, while we assumed he was in Salikenni tending to our students there, he was actually somewhere else. *Londi Kaffo's* story began to unravel. Several of the prominent villagers, whose names had been on the original faxed request for a breakfast program, told us their names had been used without their consent. The breakfast program was a pure hoax.

This led us to another problem involved in trying to conduct an assistance program from thousands of miles away. If you no longer trust your manager, how in the world can you find a trustworthy one?

The obvious candidate to succeed Momodou was Fatou Janneh, a veteran teacher in Gambian schools, who lived in Sukuta, in the suburbs of Banjul. I had come to know her through Momodou. He had taken me to her house several times in recent months. We had sat in her living room, discussing education. She was very interested in the details of the scholarship program and from time to time offered very useful advice. I offered her the job in a phone call, and after a few days thinking it over, she said yes.

I fired Momodou during a telephone call on January 19, 2005. The school urged us to file civil or criminal charges against him and *Londi Kaffo*. I declined. This would have required me to spend months in court visits. It would divide the village between those loyal to Momodou and those loyal to the school. So I thanked Momodou for his past service and gave him three months' severance pay.

"Who's going to manage the scholarships?" he asked in the phone call.

"We have hired Fatou Janneh," I said.

"I'll talk to her about it," Momodou replied. "You know she's my legal wife. I never told you that."

I called Fatou.

"Pay no attention to Momodou," she said.

I let the subject drop.

It turned out that Momodou and Fatou Janneh had, indeed, been married for a brief time. When we hired her, the marriage already was a thing of the past.

It is fair to say that Momodou, despite his larcenous streak, gave much to SSF during its formative years. He had a genuine passion for educating young people, including some on whom most educators would give up. He and I had spent a great deal of time traveling between Salikenni and the Kombos and the surrounding area, waiting for hours on lonely roadsides for a commercial van to come along, walking long distances when none came. He's now principal of a school in the North Bank area. I often stop at his father's compound in Salikenni to say hello, and I have found Momodou there a few times. We have a cordial relationship.

———◆•◆•◆———

Fatou Janneh, who became SSF's manager in The Gambia in February 2005, is both a traditional African woman and a very modern one. She's small and slender and wears ankle-length dresses and a headscarf.

Fatou Janneh.

She grew up in Sukuta, a big commercial and residential suburb of Banjul. Her father was a farmer and fisherman. Neither of her parents was educated. The family was poor. She was the youngest of three children. Neither of her two older brothers, Momodou and Basiru, went to school. But her parents decided to give Fatou an education. As a child she loved to read. She attended primary and middle schools in Sukuta, then Gambia Senior Secondary School in Banjul. She would board a bus in Sukuta at 5 a.m. and not get home until 8 p.m. On non-school days she helped her mother sell vegetables at a local market. After high school she enrolled in the free teacher-training program at Gambia College and earned a certificate to teach at the high school level. She taught English at the Sukuta middle school for many years, and became head of its English department and later vice-principal.

When Fatou agreed to join our program she was teaching English full-time at Koto Senior Secondary School outside Banjul and was also attending the University of The Gambia, working for a bachelor's degree in education, which she completed in 2006. Later she left teaching and became a senior education officer in the Gambian Ministry of Higher Education, Research, Science and Technology. In that capacity, she took part in many workshops and meetings that were part of Gambian governmental efforts to improve the country's primary and secondary education, including changes in curriculum and training programs for existing teachers.

For the next seven years, Fatou's home in Sukuta was the Gambian headquarters of SSF. When I first visited her, the main street through the neighborhood was an uneven strip of sand, with impoverished shops scattered along each side. When it rained there were huge lakes in the street. Even in dry weather, trucks and vans rocked slowly along, veering from the right side to the left

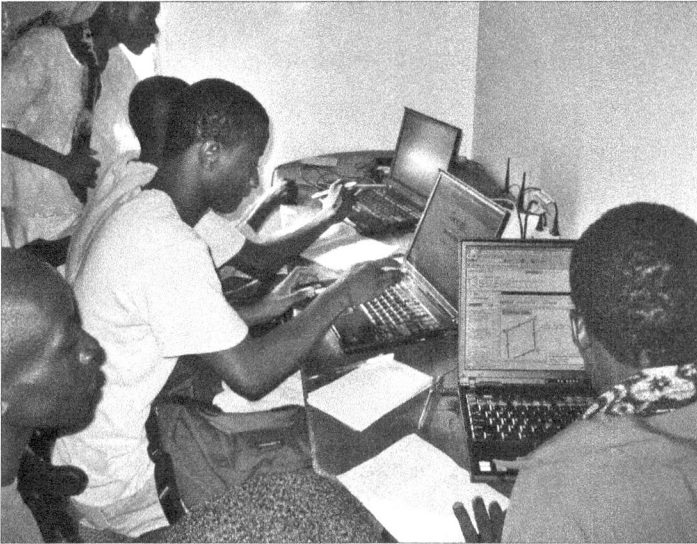

High school students using SSF computers at the former Sukuta location.

side and back again to avoid the softest sand and deepest gulleys. A few years ago, the government paved the street and installed curbs and sidewalks on both sides and a row of tall streetlights. This led, in a very short time, to an economic upsurge. Existing owners repainted their shops in bright colors with decorative signs. New shops sprang up in the gaps between the old ones. Now, day and night the sidewalks are full of people, and there is an atmosphere of optimism in the air.

Fatou's compound is on a quieter, mostly residential, sand street one block from this commercial street and running parallel to it. The compound is screened by a high masonry wall. The entrance is right next to the Cheap Shop, which sells sugar, packaged food and other items. You enter the compound by climbing up a short, steep concrete slope, instead of steps, and pushing hard against a black iron gate, which makes loud complaining noises as it opens.

Inside there is a wide open space of sand and, in its center, a modest but attractive, one-story, pale yellow house. There is a small shed that serves as an extra bedroom for the compound. Another small building is the back of a tailor shop, which opens onto the street. Behind Fatou's house there is a sandy open area, shaded by several big orange trees. There is a tiny kitchen shed, just big enough to allow one person to stand. At the very rear of the compound there is another tall masonry wall, which blocks the view of a hideous neighborhood dump, where huge vulture-like birds soar and swoop. On rare occasions smoldering fires at the dump spread pungent smoke over the whole neighborhood; more often, a cool, fresh breeze wafts through the orange trees.

The house is comfortably furnished. You go down one step into a sunken living room, with a floor of big square tiles. There are two dark red, soft couches, two similar armchairs and a low, glass-topped table. The house includes two smallish bedrooms and a bathroom with cold running water. Another room is for study and dining, with two big tables, a cupboard containing years of kids' homework, a tall refrigerator that seems to lean a little more to one side every year, and in one corner a propane tank and burner that is mainly used to heat water to make tea. All major cooking is done in the little shed out back.

In this house, as a single mother, Fatou has raised four children, while also caring for her aged and frail mother. The eldest child, Aisatou, born in 1994, is a very poised young woman who speaks very precise and very correct English. When I last saw her she was in the University of The Gambia's medical school under a government scholarship. Next came Bubacarr (born in 1997), known as Buba, a husky, well-spoken boy, and two girls, Maimuna (born in 2000) and then another, Maimuna (born in 2004), whom the family calls Aji. Fatou has managed to send all her children to good schools.

Fatou inherited the compound from her father. She once told me that her first husband insisted she transfer the title to him. She refused and, as she put it, "That was the end of that marriage." She and I seldom mentioned Momodou.

One of Fatou's first steps as manager was to contact all our students in the metropolitan area and invite them to her home. They had never before met as a group. She organized weekend classes for these students in English and math, the two subjects that most of them found hardest and that repeatedly prevented many of them from rising from one level of school to another.

On Saturdays and Sundays, hours before the first students arrived for these classes, I would find Fatou in her kitchen shed cooking a big lunch for them. A wood fire burned on the cement floor. A big pot of rice rested directly on top of the burning sticks. With barely room to stand, inches from the fire, Fatou stirred the pot with a long spoon. She wore her oldest clothes. Beads of sweat stood out on her forehead. I asked her many times over the years why she didn't let us hire a cook for these meals. "I'm used to it," she would say. She employed a maid, who did other chores, but she seldom let the maid cook lunch for the students. Everything had to be done her way. Early in her tenure we hired first one and then another assistant to help Fatou. In each case, she gave them absolutely nothing to do, and they left.

The students began arriving for the tutoring classes on Saturdays and Sundays around 1 p.m. They came on beat-up bicycles and on foot, some having made multiple transfers from one jitney van route to another. Most were in high schools that were scattered around the metropolitan area. A few had failed grade nine in Salikenni and were repeating the grade in a metropolitan school, usually at our expense. Several were in technical or business colleges. The students sat on plastic chairs under the orange trees at the rear of the compound. They congregated in small bunches. The girls usually huddled together separately. Students who had been assigned English homework scribbled in their exercise books to finish up. The students compared their notes, and talked in low voices and laughed. They filled zebra-striped teakettles with water from a tap in the compound and did their religious ablutions. They spread mats on the ground and prayed in small groups in the Muslim fashion. Around 3 p.m. Fatou, or more often one of her children, would place directly on the ground a heaping basin of rice, topped with pieces of fish or chicken or beef, with a steaming sauce. The students gathered around, some pulling up their chairs, others squatting on their heels. Some had been given spoons. But most ate in the Gambian way, with the fingers of their right hand. They ate mostly in silence, sometimes exchanging a few quiet words. In moments the entire basin would be empty. Fatou, meanwhile, bathed and changed clothes in the house. She emerged very prim in a long gown and headscarf and walked with the students a short distance down the sand street to a nearby primary school where the weekend classes were held. Later, Fatou bought a big whiteboard and held the classes under her orange trees.

A teacher from a Kombos high school was hired to teach the math classes. Fatou herself conducted the English classes. These included basic grammar and spelling with a heavy emphasis on writing and speaking. She and the class would pick a topic for an essay. In back and forth discussion they identified the elements that should go into it, and these were written on the board. They would discuss an outline. Then Fatou would send them off with instructions to write an essay and bring it the following week for her to review. Students often read their essays in class. This was a kind of teaching often missing from the schools the students attended, and one that had never been part of our program before. Because the students were at such different levels—from grade nine repeaters to university students—Fatou had to divide the classes into subgroups. While one group wrote an assignment, she engaged the other in discussion. At the end of each class, Fatou reimbursed the students for their two-way fare that day.

When Fatou first began these weekend classes only a few students attended. Some of our students were loyal to Momodou and felt we should not have fired him. Some felt we should have hired a new manager from Salikenni. Gradually, however, more and more students showed up. In time, a majority attended regularly. The few who did not show up were usually failing students.

Soon, it became clear that more was going on in these weekend classes than remedial tutoring. Fatou was instilling in her students a sense that they belonged to a special group. On a number of occasions I heard students speak of themselves as a "family." More than one commented to me over the years that Fatou was "like a mother to us."

But Fatou also was a stern disciplinarian. She required all students to bring their school results to her at the end of each term. She had a veteran teacher's talent for spotting an altered school report or a phony excuse. But if a student really needed help she would go to great lengths to provide it. She bought books for individual students. She went to their schools to work out problems

A meeting of SSF students in Fatou Janneh's compound in Sukuta in 2011.

with teachers and principals. On at least two occasions she invited a student to live in the little furnished shed in her compound and to share meals and companionship with her family.

In addition, she urged the students to form small study groups among those who lived or went to school in the same areas, and for students who were strong in a particular subject to work with those who were struggling with the subject.

It was during Fatou's years that our senior students began taking on a more active role in the program. By the fall of 2010 we had seven students in the University of The Gambia and two in local colleges. Abdoulie Bah and Mariama Ceesay began making trips to Salikenni to tutor our students there. Modou Lamin Darboe helped the outside math teacher conduct weekend classes and, when necessary, conducted these classes himself. Ousman Jarju and others kept in touch with many of our students and informed

Fatou and me of their problems. The students gave us valuable advice on the running of the program. In October of 2011 Ousman chaired a meeting of all our Kombos students, at the secondary and university levels, under Fatou's orange trees. The main theme of the meeting was the need for students to help each other. "If you are good at English, help the ones who are not good," said Ebrima Fatty, our agricultural student. "This program is entirely our own," said Ousman. "Let us help one another." Fatou sat quietly and allowed the students to shape the meeting.

In the summer of 2006 Alison and I invited Fatou to visit us in Vermont for two weeks. I wrote a letter to the U.S. Embassy in Banjul explaining the nature of the visit: It would be a reward for her good work, an opportunity for us to confer with our manager, and a chance for her to meet some of our contributors, visit schools in our area, and meet some American teachers. The letter stressed that she was a professional woman, a divorced mother of four children and a property owner. (She held a 99-year lease on her home compound.) We paid the $100 fee for her visa application.

Fatou was given a date for an interview and showed up at the embassy with a copy of our letter and all her documents. When her turn came she stood before a consular officer. He didn't invite her to sit. He glanced at her application and at our letter. Then he handed her a form letter and said, "Next person." The form letter said, "Dear Applicant: We regret to inform you that you have been found ineligible for a nonimmigrant visa under Section 214(b) of the Immigration and Nationality Act." That section reads in part: "Every alien shall be presumed to be an immigrant until he establishes to the satisfaction of the officer, at the time of the application for a visa . . . that he is entitled to nonimmigrant status." It also states that an applicant must "demonstrate strong ties" to career, home and family. In other words, the burden of proof is on the applicant to show that she would return to her country at the end of the visit.

Fatou felt humiliated. Alison and I were ashamed for our country. We enlisted the help of Senator Patrick Leahy, a Democrat from Vermont, who urged the embassy to reconsider. I traveled to The Gambia and met with officials in the political branch of the embassy. They suggested that Fatou reapply (for another $100) and said they would make a positive recommendation to the consular section of the embassy. On this second try, Fatou's visitor's visa was approved.

We met Fatou's plane at the Baltimore-Washington International Airport outside Washington, D.C. The next day we showed her around the nation's capital. She found the Lincoln Memorial a moving experience. She already was familiar with Lincoln's story and with the speech that Martin Luther King gave there. We drove with her to visit our friends in Poughkeepsie, New York, stopping on the way at the Franklin D. Roosevelt Presidential Library and Museum in Hyde Park. After we arrived in Norwich, Vermont, we introduced her to several of our donors and took her to visit a number of local schools. Between these engagements she loved to sit in a rocking chair on our front porch reading *The New York Times.*

Looking back, Fatou said that what she remembered most were many of the small things: The roads "were not broken." The grass, as we drove along, was so green. The schools were so well-equipped. In one primary class that we visited with her, there was a laptop computer for each child. The houses were so huge. People were so friendly.

With her family to take care of, a demanding professional career, the weekend classes and endless administrative duties for SSF, Fatou was not able to spend much time in Salikenni. I think also that she felt uneasy there because it was the hometown of her former husband, Momodou. But she managed to go there several times each year for a few days at a time. On these visits she would call our Salikenni students together in groups. She held large meetings with the parents of our students, urging them to become involved in their children's education. She met with school officials and village committees.

Fatou paid special attention to the girls in our program; on her trips to the village she always arranged a separate meeting with the SSF girls. She told them there was no limit to what they could make of their lives if they stuck to their education. She warned them against pregnancy and early marriage. She told them: "Husbands come and go, but education lasts forever." She was always on the lookout for older girls that she could bring into the program in high school or beyond, partly to use them as role models for the younger girls.

On visits to the village she made our process of selecting grade seven students more professional. Our selection criteria have always been financial need and academic ability. It was on Fatou's initiative that we began testing applicants in math, reading and writing, to better measure their ability.

On October 22, 2012, SSF came to a sudden turning point: Fatou sent us a brief email saying the Gambian government had given her a scholarship for a year's study at Manchester Metropolitan University in England to earn a master's degree in educational leadership and management. I called her at her office to congratulate her. She said her course had already started and therefore she would leave very soon. She said we could continue to hold the weekend classes in her compound and keep our computers there. I phoned Ousman and asked him if he would take over as interim manager. He immediately agreed, on one condition: He wanted to ask the other senior students to form a management team to help him.

I called Fatou and told her we could not afford to continue her salary and also pay a salary to Ousman, and that we would therefore consider her to be on unpaid leave until she returned. She promised to send us her financial accounting and various student reports before she left. That was the last I heard from her directly. I learned from Ousman that she had met with him for an hour and given him the SSF checkbook. Two weeks later, her daughter, Aisatou, informed us that Fatou had left the country. She never gave us an accounting statement, and she left arrangements for several students unclear.

Alison and I made the decision that we would not invite Fatou to return as manager. We dropped the word "interim" from Ousman's title.

Within a few days, we learned that Fatou had moved her children and her mother out of the Sukuta compound and rented it to a family that none of us knew. We worried about the security of our computers. Ousman and his team quickly moved them to a room in his compound in Fajikunda.

During her tenure Fatou contributed hugely to the SSF program. It was under Fatou that our students began calling themselves a family. She brought to the program a degree of professionalism that we never had before. She raised the entire operation to a level that allowed the new board of senior students to take over seamlessly. The team at that point faced many challenges. One of these, which deserves a chapter of its own, was how to run a successful scholarship program in the environment of a Gambian school system, which itself is suffering severe growing pains.

CHAPTER 5

A Gambian Education

MONDAY, APRIL 15, 2013, was the first day of school after a two-week recess, but the Salikenni school was absent. It was truant. There was no education going on.

The buildings were there—the decrepit blocks of classrooms for the primary grades, with faded whitewashed walls and rusty, corrugated metal roofs; and, just behind these, an L-shaped row of drab, somewhat newer buildings for grades seven through nine, known as the upper school. The principal's house was there—a box-like pile of masonry that resembles a military guard post. The SSF-maintained library was there—one of the few bright spots on the entire campus, white with green iron shutters. Our librarian, Fatou Darboe, was there at 8:30 a.m. sharp, sweeping the linoleum floor and straightening the books on the shelves.

Outside the school, on a masonry wall next to the entrance, the familiar mural was there, proclaiming: "Welcome to the Salikenni Basic Cycle School, Est. in 1951." It shows a woman in a green dress, labeled "Unknown Mother of Excellence," and a man, labeled "Unknown Father of Success," and a boy running. It bears the motto: "Discipline—Hard Work—Success."

The wavy banner on the Salikenni school sign reads "Discipline—Hard Work—Success." The man is labeled "Unknown Father of Success," the woman, "Unknown Mother of Excellence."

But at the start of the school day only one teacher was present out of the staff of about 18. He was Omar K. Dibba, who was teaching upper school math. Dibba, then 28, grew up in Albreda, in the area depicted in the book *Roots*. He went through grade nine there, then to high school in Esau, a North Bank village near the terminal of the ferry from Banjul. He earned a primary teacher certificate at Gambia College, and later a higher teacher certificate, all at government expense. He was now in his second year teaching math in Salikenni. He told me he did not consider teaching to be his life's career. He soon would be looking for "broader horizons."

Instead of about 700 students in the lower and upper schools combined, there were, on this opening day, perhaps 50. A dozen of them went to the library and either read or just chatted with one another. Some found shady spots in the sand schoolyard to

The Salikenni schoolyard bustles with activity once the school reaches its momentum after inevitably slow starts following holidays.

sit together and wait. Others hung around a short time and then went out into the village. The principal, Sainey Fatajo, was at the school, but he made no attempt to gather the students together, or give them a welcome back speech, or tell them when classes might resume. Later in the morning, Foday Camara, a grade six teacher, showed up. He and Dibba were the only two teachers to arrive the entire first day. Camara found about a dozen grade six students and held a class for them. Dibba later in the day conducted a math class for a smattering of upper school students.

Dibba commented that a slow start at the beginning of a new term was "a Gambian tradition." He said it would be a week or more before the school would have a full complement of teachers and students. He was stating the obvious. SSF had seen the same thing happen at this school for years, at the start of every school year and after every long holiday. It was not peculiar to The Gambia. Former Peace Corps volunteers in other African countries told me they observed the same thing. The principal explained that some of his teachers were attending a government workshop on phonics in a nearby town; others were working on The Gambia decennial census, which was then getting under way; others had simply decided to extend their holiday by a week or more. As it turned out, it did take a week and a half for the school to achieve near-normal operation.

Physically, on the opening Monday, the school was a shambles. In the primary school section not one classroom had been made ready for students. One classroom contained several tables, but the chairs were still locked in a storeroom; another was equipped with wrought-iron desk-bench combinations—each long enough for three or four small students—but, during the holidays, someone had pried the plywood desktops off every unit, leaving only the

With no textbooks in the school, a teacher writes an entire lesson on the board. This is one of the school's more modern classrooms for grades seven through nine.

metal frames with nothing to write on. Principal Fatajo explained that the older buildings in the school were not equipped with locks.

Two days later a few more teachers and students arrived. I dropped in on Kebba Jallow's grade nine science class to observe his teaching. As I entered, Jallow was writing a lesson about the human respiratory system on the blackboard. He wrote in a tight, even script, starting high up on the left corner of the board. He held a battered, dog-eared pamphlet in his left hand, from which he was copying the lesson. The students were supposed to copy what he wrote into their exercise books. When Jallow had filled up the left half of the board, he moved to the right half. Then he erased the left half and resumed writing there. Many of the students struggled to keep up with him. The topic on which he wrote changed to the nervous system. When he came to a diagram of the human brain, he handed the pamphlet to a student, chosen for his artistic talent, who very slowly and deliberately reproduced the diagram on the board. I noticed that several students didn't bother copying it but were chatting quietly among themselves. "I have a pamphlet," one explained. "I have that diagram." When the diagram on the board was complete, Jallow, consulting his battered pamphlet, drew arrows next to the diagram on the board, naming several parts of the brain. Then someone outside rang a hand-held bell, and the class was over. During the entire time that I was there, Jallow said not a word.

Jallow, 28 at the time, had graduated from Gambia College's teacher-training program in 2007. This was his first year at the Salikenni school. He was teaching both general science and agriculture to grades one through nine. He said he had absolutely no science equipment—no microscope, no Bunsen burner, no

As their teacher writes, students struggle to copy down every word.

flasks. But he had learned at the college how to improvise basic experiments using water bottles and tin cans and plastic tubes. He told me that he would return, in a later class, to the anatomy lesson he had put on the board, at which point there would be a classroom discussion about it.

———◆◆◆———

I have sat in on other classes, in math and English, during which there was a lively back-and-forth discussion between teacher and students. But the system of teaching-by-copying is still one of the main methods used in the Salikenni school, the reason being that in recent years there have been virtually no textbooks available in the school.

Long ago the Gambian school system tried to provide free textbooks to each student, but the costs of reprinting new ones each year were high. The World Bank stepped in and devised a textbook rental system for the country's schools. Parents paid a book rental fee on top of the school fee. The books were to be returned at the end of each year. The idea was that children would take better care of their books if they paid for them, and the government then would not have to print so many. It didn't work. Many parents paid only the school fee, with the result that many students had no books. In 2007 the rental system was abandoned, and the Gambian government announced it would provide textbooks free to every child for whom the school fee had been paid. But there have been breakdowns in the system of supply.

In October 2011, I and Mary Ann Roberts and Bill Babcock, two American supporters of SSF, learned that almost no student in the upper school had a textbook in any subject. Incredibly we found that many boxes of textbooks had been locked in a storage cabinet. The school had not distributed them because the number of books supplied by the government had been less than half the amount needed. Mary Ann persuaded the principal that half the required number of books in the hands of students would be better than none. We spent two days helping to distribute the books, one for every two students to share, except in grade eight where it had to be one for each three or four students.

Now, in April 2013, I again found that no student in the upper school had been issued a textbook. The principal and the regional education office in Kerewan said that a complete set of newly revised textbooks was "on order," but no one knew when the books might arrive. The principal did have a quantity of supplemental textbooks—

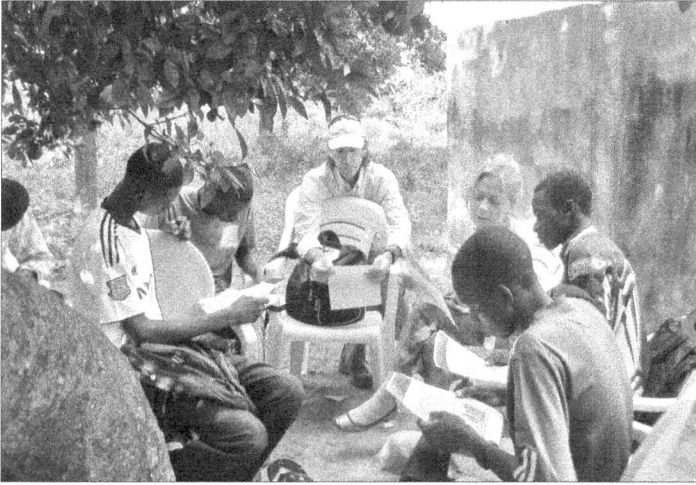

Mary Ann Roberts and Bill Babcock meeting with SSF students in Sukuta in 2011.

not the official ones but covering similar ground. But there were not enough to distribute, so he had placed them in the library.

During that same visit, I chatted with Bubacarr Fatajo, a bright, articulate boy newly admitted to SSF in grade seven in Salikenni. I asked him what he would like to do after he finished his education. "I would like to be a bank manager," he replied. Never mind that a few months earlier he had told Mary Ann he wanted to be a doctor. Here was a boy with big ideas. His grandmother, Mama Ceesay, a very thin woman whose face bore the wrinkles of decades in the rice fields, said she hoped at least three children in the extended family would eventually attend the university. She said she was strict about the children's study habits. She never allowed them to go out and play after dinner. She insisted they "read their books" every evening. Bubacarr used the same phrase: "I read my books." I asked him if he could show me some of the books he read. He went into the house and came out with three of them. All three were his exercise books, containing the notes he had copied from blackboards.

Ousman Jarju and his management team also had observed the lack of textbooks. As soon as they had sufficient funds, they visited bookstalls in Banjul and bought supplementary textbooks in each of the core subjects and distributed them to each of our students. The titles had been recommended to us by Salikenni teachers, who said they were generally better than those provided by the education ministry.

And though the school lacked textbooks, it appeared to have a full complement of qualified teachers—a marked difference from my earlier trips when I had witnessed acute shortages of teachers.

In November 2008, there was no English teacher for grades seven through nine—a third-grade teacher was filling in. There should have been two science teachers, but there was only one. There was no home economics teacher. As I walked by a grade nine home economics class, the students were doing stretching exercises. I walked into a grade nine class in social and environmental studies (SES), which also had no teacher, and found that Haruna Jallow, a student, was at the blackboard teaching his classmates. Haruna was then the "head boy" of the school, an elected office similar to student council president. Haruna was writing on the board: "An eclipse is the obscuring of light of either the sun or the moon." He was not copying from a textbook. There was not a single textbook in the room. Haruna was copying from the exercise book of another student known for taking good notes. These notes were from an earlier class. With zero teaching experience, I tried to demonstrate an eclipse of the sun. I made Haruna, with his bright green head boy shirt, the sun; others, the earth and moon. I got them circling properly, and then stopped the action to show at a given point that the earth could not see the sun. The students said they understood. (A year later, Haruna was admitted to the SSF program. More on him later.)

The Salikenni school also suffered—and still does—from an acute lack of teaching materials. There were no science tools; in most of the classrooms the walls were bare. In 2007, I brought two microscopes that had been donated by schools in the Upper Valley of New Hampshire and Vermont. The microscopes were of low magnification, but Alfusainy Jatta, who then taught science, immediately began using them to show students grains of sand, the surface of a seemingly smooth stone and the veins in a leaf. One of the U.S. schools had also given us an inflatable dinosaur. The dinosaur, a cuddly tyrannosaurus, was an instant hit, but also a mystery. One teacher, not a science teacher, speculated that it might be an animal we currently have in America. I explained that dinosaurs lived on earth "millions and millions" of years ago, that they probably expired in a natural disaster and that their compressed remains are part of the petroleum that we use today. A commercial van passed by at that moment, and I suggested it was running on old dinosaurs. Jatta was fascinated. He found a book about dinosaurs in the library and began including the subject in his classes. Sadly, the microscopes and the dinosaur have long ago disappeared. And Jatta is no longer teaching at the school.

During her 2007 visit to the school, Alison attended a first-grade class and found herself in the role of assistant teacher. "I guided a child's hand on the blackboard to show him how to write the letter s," she wrote. "Suddenly all the other kids crowded around, wanting to do the same thing, pushing us against the blackboard. A student copied a lesson from the blackboard perfectly—but in mirror image. There may be many students with learning disabilities, but I saw no services. In a school of 700 students I saw no student wearing glasses."

Many things have changed since the days when teachers went out with drummers to persuade parents to send their children to school. We have repeatedly seen in our program how highly most village parents now value education. A year before she left, Fatou Janneh and I went to Salikenni to select a new group of students to admit to SSF in grade seven. We were looking for five girls and five boys who would meet our entry criteria—financial need and evidence of academic promise. We hired the town crier to announce that parents who wished to apply on behalf of their children should come to the library at 9 a.m. the following morning, a Wednesday, when village residents would normally not go to their farms. The crier, Lamin Colly, a young man who also was the manager of the German nursery school in the village, went around the village with a hand-held, battery-powered loudspeaker that also contained a very loud siren. At each main intersection he set off the siren and made the announcement. We also made mobile phone calls to extend the same invitation to parents in Dobo, Mandori and Bani, three villages within about an hour's walk from Salikenni, whose children attend the Salikenni school for parts of their education and who are equally eligible for our program.

A deluge of applications followed. Bearded farmers came in their long robes, fingering strings of prayer beads. Several women walked seven kilometers from Dobo with babies tied in shawls on their backs, and nursed them while waiting to be interviewed. Slightly more women than men came on behalf of their children. Soon we had more than 30 applicants. People who said they had missed the news kept coming for three more days.

The next step was to interview each prospective student and conduct three brief tests: a writing test ("write a short summary of a book you have read or a story you have heard"); a reading aloud test, using a set of African stories in English graded by level of difficulty; and a simple math test.

The results provided a clear picture of the extent to which grades one through six at the Salikenni school had prepared children for middle school. On the essay question many could do no more than rewrite the question verbatim. Some could not read the first level of our African stories. In math, most had little understanding of units, tens, hundreds and thousands. Asked to write the number 4023 in words, many wrote "four hundred and twenty." Gambian currency is divided into hundredths, like many others. One dalasi equals 100 bututs. But many of our applicants could not answer the question, "100 bututs equals how many dalasis?" Even fewer could answer the question, "3.5 dalasis equals how many bututs?"

The boys, on average, did much better than the girls. We quickly identified seven boys who did fairly well on the tests. But only one girl scored in the same range as these boys. If we had followed the test results alone we would have chosen mostly boys. But as Fatou reiterated: "We don't want this to be a boys' program. Our goal is also to educate girls." So we took in seven qualified boys and seven mostly underqualified girls.

The majority of the parents of SSF students are illiterate. While they want their children to be educated, few are able to be mentors in that education. They can't read them stories or help them in their schoolwork. I remember one boy, whom I'll call Ahmed, who several years ago had been in grade seven in Salikenni. He was apparently talented, but he had missed several weeks of school. I went with a teacher to see his father, a thin, frail, old man in a brown robe that needed washing. The father said he was no longer able to do much work, and he depended on Ahmed. It was Ahmed who kept the farm going, he said, and who climbed the baobab tree and cut the branches that threatened to fall on the house in the next storm. The father told us he very much wanted Ahmed to be educated, but he hadn't realized that this would mean going to school every day. He seemed to think our scholarship would automatically turn into an education. He promised to give his son time to attend school and study at home. Ahmed returned to classes, but the next year he did not show up for school, and we never heard from him again.

And I well recall another father who was very proud that his daughter was in high school. When I informed him that his daughter was failing every subject, he replied, "I never knew."

While they may not be individual mentors, Salikenni parents, along with those in the nearby villages, can come together as a political force for education, and in fact have formed a parent-teacher association. In the fall of 2010 I attended a raucous meeting of this PTA group in the Salikenni schoolyard. Several dozen men and women, dressed in their finest, sat in a circle on plastic chairs in the shade of the big neem tree.

One after another, in long speeches, they complained about the quality of education at the school. They said the school was not

A parents' meeting at Saikenni school. The building at rear is the library.

preparing students to pass the exam leading to high school. The failure rate was too high. They pointed out that more than a month after the start of the school year there was no math teacher for grades seven through nine; there was no arts and crafts teacher; there were not enough textbooks. One speaker said that the Salikenni school had once been one of the best in the region, but now it was "one of the worst."

━━━━━◆◆◆◆━━━━━

One of the biggest challenges facing the Salikenni school as well as other Gambian schools has been the teaching of English. Since independence from British colonial rule in 1965, English has been the official language of The Gambia. It is the language of education. Beyond the first few primary grades, most of the teaching in Gambian schools is done in English. Gambian government reports are written in English. Monthly bank statements are in English. English is the language in which students must have some fluency in order to get into high school, and even more mastery to enter the university. For Gambians who want to get ahead, the colonial language is a necessity.

But English is not the language in which Gambian mothers sing to their babies, or in which infants utter their first words, or children speak on the playground. In Salikenni that language is Mandinka. Only a few Salikenni parents—the younger ones who have been to school—speak English. Among grandparents even fewer speak as much as a word of English. There are very few books in Mandinka, so when children are introduced to reading, it has to be in English.

Salikenni schoolchildren are trying to learn English from teachers who themselves often do not speak it very well. The government's grammar textbooks—even when available—appear forbidding to many students. Livelier English language textbooks that we have put in our library and sometimes have given to individual students do not seem to be widely read. During lunch hour or on the playground, students speak to each other in Mandinka. Over the years, a few Salikenni principals have tried to require students to speak only English on the school grounds, even imposing small fines for each Mandinka word. But these edicts never lasted long.

The English spoken by our students is full of little oddities, which I personally like but which the graders of exams do not. For example, they say, "Please borrow me your pen." Mandinka does not have separate words for he and she, and many of our students mix these up. They are also often thrown by the question endings: "Lamin is smart, isn't he?" or, "Lamin is not in school today, is he?" Why is the back end of the sentence negative when the front end is positive, and vice versa, they ask. I have to admit to our students that this is totally indefensible.

※

Grade nine is a critical year for Gambian students. In May and June grade nine students throughout the country take an examination that determines their eligibility to go on to high school. The exam is administered by the West African Examinations Council, which is based in Ghana. The WAEC dates back to colonial times. It was set up in 1952 to conduct exams in what were then four British colonies—Nigeria, Sierra Leone, the Gold Coast (which became Ghana), and The Gambia. Liberia was added in 1974.

In Salikenni the entire ninth-grade year is mostly a cram course for the exam. The WAEC publishes answers to questions asked in previous years. Teachers write these on the blackboards and drill them into students. There is a large selection of these questions and answers in the SSF library at the school, and, as the date of the exam approaches, students go to the library, sometimes in groups of four or five, and pore over them. SSF tutoring classes in English and math for grade nine students in Salikenni are aimed at the exam. A number of teachers at the school have their own tutoring classes after school, especially for ninth graders. Some charge a fee; others do it for free.

The examination process takes place at the Salikenni school over a period of about two weeks; there are between seven and nine separate exams. Students must do them in the four core subjects—English, math, general science and social studies. Other subjects are optional, if the school teaches them.

A soccer game during recess at the Salikenni school, with sticks for goalposts.

An outside monitor, usually a principal or teacher from another school, is sent to the village to supervise the exams. One year we believe an unscrupulous Salikenni principal persuaded the examiner to look the other way while Salikenni teachers entered the test room and coached some students. A number of SSF students, who got very good exam scores that year, failed miserably when they reached high school.

The exams are graded by the WAEC. (Fatou Janneh was often among the graders in English.) The results are tallied in what, to Americans, is an upside-down way. Each subject is scored on a scale of 1 to 9, where 1 is excellent and 9 is a failure. Results for the four core subjects plus the best two among the optional subjects are then added together to create an "aggregate" score. The best overall score mathematically possible is aggregate 6 (1×6). The worst possible is aggregate 54 (9×6).

In recent years the Gambian school system has considered 42 or below to be the cutoff mark for eligibility to high school. However, some high schools in the government system use their own cutoff marks, which may be around 30 for most students, or around 20 for students applying for the science curriculum. Some schools will admit students with scores above 42 in certain cases. Family influence and favoritism of one kind or another are not unknown in The Gambia.

After taking the grade nine exam, students have an agonizing wait before learning their results. Often these are not made public until after the start of the school year in September. Then there is a chaotic rush to enroll in high school. Many students with marginal scores have to go from school to school looking for a place. As a result, it can take a few weeks for a tenth-grade class in a big metropolitan area high school to actually get down to the business of education.

The WAEC's ninth-grade exam has brought the education of many Salikenni students, including those in SSF, to a sudden halt. For example, in 2009, 61 ninth graders took the exam at the Salikenni village school. Only ten passed, all of them boys. Not a single girl passed. Of the total who took the exam, 14 were our scholarship students—seven boys and seven girls. Four of our boys passed. None of our girls passed. (For more on this gender disparity, see Chapter 7, Educating Girls.) In 2010 and 2011 the success rates for both boys and girls, in the entire ninth grade and for those in our program, were not much better.

But in 2012 and again in 2013, the results for SSF's grade nine students suddenly turned completely around. In each of those years nine SSF students, including five girls, took the grade nine exam, and every one of them passed. They are all now in high school. Several factors may have been at work in this rather dramatic improvement:

- The Salikenni school seems to have been doing a better job in the last two years teaching two difficult subjects, English and math.
- Our tutoring of SSF students in Salikenni seems to be paying off.
- We have hired the school's English and math teachers to hold after-school classes for our students.
- Some of our senior students have tutored in Salikenni during their own holiday breaks.
- Our selection process now does a better job of seeking out qualified students who are in financial need.
- In meetings with students and other meetings with parents, we have tried to spread the message that these students can rise to any height if they try.

When the 2012 results came out, we wondered whether cheating had played a role in the improved exam scores. We noted that several of the students who did well on the grade nine exam performed very poorly when they reached grade ten. But the good results two years in a row make us doubt that cheating was involved. And the poor showing of some students starting grade ten seems to be the result of the transition to a new environment. (See Chapter 9.)

Some Gambians have long complained that the WAEC is too strict with its grading. However, we have found over the years that this exam is a very good predictor of success or failure in high school. When our students fail the exam by one or two points, we ask them to repeat grade nine, usually in a middle school in the metropolitan area. Sometimes they refuse to repeat, and their families pull religious or political strings to get high schools to accept them. These students usually fail in high school, and we drop them from our funding.

In 2009 Momodou L. Fatajo, the son of a Salikenni fisherman and farmer, got an aggregate 46 on the exam (far on the wrong side of the cutoff of 42). He searched for a high school in the Kombos, but none would take him. Fatou Janneh and I urged him to repeat ninth grade at a Kombos school. His Kombos guardian, Haruna Fatajo, was at first opposed to this but finally agreed. Momodou repeated grade nine at Bakoteh Upper Basic School in the Kombos and this time passed with a rather good 32. He was admitted to St. Augustine Senior Secondary in downtown Banjul in 2010–11. He completed high school in 2013 and began an access course to improve some of his exam results. At last word, he hoped soon to enroll in the university.

One striking pattern in Gambian education—which actually is typical of virtually all low-income African countries—is a decline in enrollment at each higher level. A 2011 study conducted by the World Bank, UNESCO and the Gambian Ministry of Basic and Secondary Education and reported in the Gambia Education Country Status Report (page 82) calculated that, of 100 children starting grade one, 67 would reach grade seven, 38 would reach grade ten and 26 would reach grade twelve. We have seen a similar pattern of attrition in our own program. From 1996, when SSF began, through 2012, 207 students entered the program. Of these, 62 completed high school, 27 went on to higher education, 91 dropped out on their own or were dropped by us for failing grades, and 54 were still in the program in grades seven through twelve.

The biggest number of dropouts occurred in the early years of the program and involved failing the grade nine exam.

⬥•◦•◦•⬥

The Gambian constitution stipulates: "Basic education shall be free, compulsory and available to all." The Gambia officially defines a "basic education" to be grades one through nine. This combined goal has long been assumed to be unachievable in the foreseeable future. But the Gambian government now says it's going to implement it.

On July 27, 2013, Gambian President Yahya Jammeh announced that, starting in September 2014, education would be free in grades one through nine for all children throughout the country. The first step took place in September 2013, when the government discontinued school fees for the primary grades. These fees were relatively small, and most families could afford them.

In an interview with Ousman Jarju and me in November 2013, Baboucarr Buoy, Permanent Secretary for Basic and Secondary Education, described the more significant second step. Starting in September 2014, he said, parents will pay only for exercise books, pens, pencils, uniforms, lunches and grade nine examination fees. Beginning in the fall of 2015, the government has proposed to partially subsidize high school education for students.

Buoy said he was unable to give us an estimate of how much these changes would increase enrollment, how many new classrooms would have to be built, how many more teachers would be needed, and how much it would all cost or exactly where the money would come from. He said the government would pay for the first year, and then it hoped the World Bank would come in.

I left the interview rather skeptical that this ambitious plan could be carried out on schedule and, if so, whether it could be sustained. At that time, the proposal had received little discussion in the major Gambian newspapers.

The Gambia Education Country Status Report, cited above, noted that The Gambia's school-age population is growing year by year. Because of this population growth, the report said (on page 62), that The Gambia, in order to achieve universal education through grade nine by 2020, will have to increase the number of seats in the school system by 70 percent.

Buoy said that once basic education became free, the government could take up the "compulsory" part of the constitutional mandate. "If it's not free," he said, "you can't make it compulsory. Now we will be able to enforce the compulsory part." He didn't suggest exactly how.

But how will all this affect SSF? Ousman and I decided we would have to wait and see. SSF has always been based on meeting a need. If the need changes we will adjust. If less money is needed for tuitions, we will have more to spend on the quality of education, and on higher education.

CHAPTER 6

The Making of a Librarian

WHEN FATOU DARBOE finished grade two, her father told her that girls were not meant to be educated and she would have to quit school. Her grandmother agreed, saying Fatou should stay home and take care of her little sister.

That might have determined the course of her life. But Fatou was very bright and inquisitive and, even at that age, ambitious. She taught herself to read and write. Years later, when SSF was looking for a librarian, she was the perfect choice.

Fatou's childhood friend Kaddy continued to attend school without Fatou. Fatou would follow her there and linger in the schoolyard and sometimes chat with teachers. Kaddy wrote out the letters A to Z for Fatou and the numbers up to 100. When Kaddy was in grade six she gave Fatou her grade three English textbook, and Fatou read it all.

A friend gave Fatou a storybook about a grumpy lion who lived in a cave. When other animals came to chat, the lion would groan and say he didn't feel well. One day a goat and a sheep went into the lion's cave, and he ate them up. Fatou has been in love with storybooks ever since. She borrowed them from people she met. (There was no library in the village then.) When she came upon a

Librarian Fatou Darboe in the Salikenni library with the ledger she uses to check books in and out.

strange word in a book, she would write it on her palm with a pen and ask a teacher what it meant.

Her grandmother disparaged her efforts. "You are always reading and writing," the old woman told her. "You don't do anything. You don't know anything."

When Fatou was a young woman, the nonprofit group Save the Children gave her a job teaching women in Salikenni to read and write in Mandinka. It was her first salary. She held the job for two years. Then the Salikenni school hired her as an "unqualified teacher." In those days it was common for schools to hire teachers with no training. She taught grade one for four years, then nursery school for two years.

In January 2009 the Gambian government decided to dismiss all uncertified teachers unless they could pass an entrance exam and go to Gambia College to become certified. With her two years of formal schooling, no one suggested that Fatou should take the exam, so she was about to lose her job.

But just at that moment the Salikenni Scholarship Fund happened to be looking for a new librarian for the library it sponsors at the school. We hired Fatou that February, and we feel it was the best decision we ever made.

The library is in an old storage building, which SSF has renovated in stages over the years. We have supplied most of the books, and we pay the salary of the librarian. The library building is owned by the school. In 2003 we sent over by ocean freight 1,000 books, donated by schools and libraries in the Upper Valley area of Vermont and New Hampshire. Some of these were strikingly irrelevant to the lives of African children. Some had opening sentences such as, "Julie jumped in her mom's station wagon to be driven to her piano lesson." Since then we have concentrated on building up the library's collection of African stories and novels by African authors. The library is the only project involving the school itself that we have continued. It is open to students, teachers and village residents. In 2007, when rural electrification reached Salikenni, we installed electricity in the library, and it has been used since then for tutoring classes with groups of students at night.

In the library's early years we had great trouble finding and keeping librarians. We arranged for a young man who had just finished high school under our program to run the library until we could find a computer course for him to attend. But that happened sooner than expected, and he served in the library only for a few months. Another short-term librarian was a young woman, a former scholarship student, who had become pregnant while in high school, dropped out, and was living in the village raising her child. There were periods between librarians when a teacher was theoretically in charge. On several visits I and others spent hours arranging the books only to return a year later and find them stuffed onto the shelves, often upside down or backwards, with books for young readers and those on history and science all jumbled together.

On her first day on the job, Fatou Darboe wasn't sure what the words fiction, biography, or reference meant. But she learned quickly, and in a very short time the books were organized and neatly shelved in their proper categories. When someone borrows a book, she records it in a big ledger and adds a checkmark when the book is returned. If it doesn't come back she goes into the classroom and confronts the borrower.

Students working in the library, 2013.

Fatou sweeps the library every morning. Her "broom" is a short bundle of straw held in her hand. The library is an oasis of cleanliness in a school of dusty, and in some cases dilapidated, classrooms. Without being told, the children step out of their flip-flops as they enter the building, leaving them spread out on the stone step outside.

When she began the job, Fatou was a slow and halting reader. But whenever she got a free moment she was reading. Often, when I was using the library as an office, Fatou would suddenly laugh and say, "This book is very funny. Listen to this." And she would read a passage aloud. She especially loved the African stories and soon knew many of them by heart. She often tells these stories to first- and second-graders in a combination of Mandinka and English, holding up the pictures for them to see.

Her own reading skills improved rapidly. Before long she could read as well or better than many of our grade nine students. Emails that she sends us, when she goes to the metropolitan area to pick up her pay, are better written than those we receive from some of our university students.

The school tends to use the library mainly in library periods. Each class, from grades one through nine, has one or more such periods each week. An entire class of 30 or 40 students will swoop in. There are a few moments of total confusion as all of them at once go to the shelves to look for a book. Then the class teacher tells them to sit and read. Some only leaf through the pages, stopping at a few of the pictures. After about 20 minutes, the students dump the books on the tables, leaving Fatou to put them back. A few give their names to Fatou and check out the books they have chosen. We have always questioned the value of these library periods. But

Bill Babcock engages SSF students in a game of flashcards in the library.

at other times of the day, when there is no big group in the library, we see students, one at a time or in twos or threes come in, look at the shelves, and select a book to take home.

During the summer of 2010, when the school and the library were closed, we enrolled Fatou in a course for rural librarians at the National Library of The Gambia in Banjul. On her first day, when the administrators of this course learned that Fatou had only a second-grade education, they sent her away. Our then manager, Fatou Janneh, explained to them that Fatou was already an experienced librarian and a good reader. They took her back, and she did very well in the course. When she received her certificate an official of the National Library told her, "Oh, Fatou. How wrong we were about you."

After taking this course, Fatou, on her own initiative, labeled all the books in the library with the Dewey Decimal System.

Fatou lives in a compound in Salikenni with her father and mother. Several brothers live there from time to time. Neither of her parents has been to school. Her father, Kebba Darboe, is thin and frail. He no longer farms. He still owns a shop, which is attached to the compound and opens onto the sand lane. He spends much of his day sitting in a plastic chair in front of the shop. But for several years there has been absolutely nothing on the shelves behind him. At other times of day he sits in the shade inside the compound with an ancient shotgun leaning against his chair. He describes the hunting trip he is about to start, but his family smiles as he does so. Fatou's mother, Serifunding, is a very thin woman who is always busy. I frequently find her pounding rice or sitting on a mat in the courtyard opening groundnut shells and sorting the nuts into different sizes and quality.

Fatou long has been the only wage earner in the family. With her library salary she put a younger brother, Ousman, through high school. Another of her brothers is Mustapha Darboe, whom SSF sponsored through middle school and high school, and in a series of journalism courses, and who later became the communications officer of the team that took over management of the scholarship program. In the SSF organization Fatou became more than our librarian, attending many of the planning meetings of the board, and working closely with the student leadership even though not an actual member of the board.

Fatou periodically gives a little money to her grandmother, the one who took part in the decision to stop her formal education in grade two. Once, when she reminded the grandmother that this money came from all the reading she had done, the old woman looked at her and said, "Fatou, you were right."

Over the years, other village women have told Fatou she should get married; in 2012 she did. Her husband was principal of a primary school in another village. He already had two wives in various parts of the country. The village women then told her she should give up the library job and go to live with her husband. She told them, "No, I would never do that. I would never give up this job." In September 2013 Fatou gave birth to a baby girl, Mariama. Her only request for maternity leave was to work only in the mornings for a few months. Other than that she didn't miss a beat in the library job.

I once asked Fatou whether there had been someone in her early life who had encouraged her to read and to learn. "No one," she replied. "I did it myself." She paused and then added, "God helped me."

Many of the readers in the SSF library pronounce each word softly to themselves as their fingers move along a line. When the library is full their voices make a steady hum, like the sound of busy bees. One day in 2009 I happened to be in the library when a class of ninth-graders stomped in for its library period. The students jostled to pick out books, but eventually they sat down and began to read. Since there were not enough chairs, some sat on the linoleum floor or on the windowsills.

I noticed one girl, one of our scholarship students—I'll call her Binta—sitting on the floor with her back against a wall. There was a book on her lap, but she was not reading it. She stared straight ahead as though her mind were far away. I invited her to an alcove in the library and asked her to read me a page from the book. It was an African story for very young children, mostly pictures with only a sentence or two on each page. She could read hardly a word. In grade nine Binta basically could not read.

How did she ever get into grade nine? A check of her record showed that in recent years she had failed most of her courses, but each year the school had promoted her to the next grade. In a few months she would take the nationwide grade nine exam that determines eligibility for high school. She couldn't possibly pass it.

Binta told me that her family was proud that she was getting an "education." She wanted to become a nurse.

We learned later that she did fail the exam, getting almost the worst score mathematically possible. At that point, given our resources, there was nothing we could do for her. We didn't offer to have her repeat, and we lost track of her.

Poor reading ability among students has long been a huge problem in Gambian schools. Some years ago the Gambia's education secretary, Fatou Lamin Faye, visited a grade seven class in a rural school and was "shocked" to discover that most of the students could not read a simple passage in English. In May 2007, her department, assisted by the World Bank, conducted reading assessments in grades one through three in 40 sample schools throughout the country.

Fatou Janneh, SSF manager at the time, was a member of one of the assessment teams. The findings were dismal: among 1,200 children tested, 99 percent could not identify the letters of the alphabet. "The result was zero," Momodou Sanneh, an official of the education ministry, recalls. "None of them could read." Further sampling showed that a large number of students in grades seven and eight and some in grade nine could not read either.

The ministry then launched an ambitious program to reform the teaching of reading in the early grades. It adopted for most Gambian schools the Jolly Phonics system, developed in the United Kingdom, which uses sounds plus hand and body motions to teach reading. The government called for testing children in grades three and five each year to monitor the system's progress.

Teachers throughout the country were trained in Jolly Phonics, and Salikenni teachers soon began using it. You could hear the change just by walking by a primary classroom. Instead of the old chant: "A, B, C . . . ," you would hear sounds like, "s-s-s-s-s," and refrains such as "I like to jump, jump, jump up and down," as a teacher pointed to the letter J and everyone jumped.

If phonics does indeed improve reading ability in Salikenni, it will take time for this to be reflected in grade nine students such as Binta.

Meanwhile, Fatou Darboe is working to improve reading skills in the library. She has organized reading classes for small groups of SSF grade seven girls. They read aloud to her. She recommends books for them to take home. When they bring the books back she discusses with them what they have read and learned. She keeps a log of books they have finished. She tells them that the way to learn to read is to read and read. She shows students how to use a dictionary. But she also tells them, "If you don't understand a word, ask someone. That's what I did. That's how I learned to read. Don't be afraid to ask."

Reading for pleasure has not been part of the culture of Salikenni and neighboring villages. A young American woman who served there in the Peace Corps, and who took along a supply of books for leisure hours, told me that the family with whom she lived always thought she was studying. "They never thought I was simply reading."

Encouraging the simple act of reading, we believe, is the most important purpose of the library. I have been in the library several times while Fatou was working with young students. I have seen her point to a sentence and smile. And then I have seen the students smile. In this way, Fatou is passing on her love of books.

CHAPTER 7

Educating Girls

AMIE DIBBA was exactly the kind of girl we have always wanted to educate. In June 2007, while Alison and I were in the village, Amie came to see us several times in the compound where we stayed. She was 17 then, a poised, self-confident young woman, able to meet and talk with us in a very open way. She had been one of our scholarship students since grade seven. Now she had just completed grade nine and was waiting for her exam results.

She saw her goals clearly. She wanted to be the first in her family to finish high school and then go to the university to become an accountant. She said she believed that education would allow a young Salikenni woman to become anything she wanted.

Her father, Momodou Bintu Dibba, a hunter and fisherman and an active member of several village committees, strongly supported Amie's education and promised to keep encouraging her. Several months later, Anne Segal, a former Peace Corps volunteer in Namibia, came with me to the village, and talked with Amie's father. He told Anne that when you educate a boy you educate one person; when you educate a girl you educate many. Anne was impressed and wrote in her trip report: "This unschooled father living in a small village in The Gambia knows what all the NGOs, with their degrees in economics and community development, have been preaching for years."

Amie did very well on the grade nine exam and, in the fall of 2007, she entered Gambia Senior Secondary School in Banjul. She lived with her stepmother, Ida Camara, in Talinding, next door to Fajikunda in the suburbs of Banjul. She shared a room with a sister and a brother.

Very quickly, however, something went wrong. Her marks in grades ten, eleven and twelve were terrible. But each year she was promoted. Gambia High once was considered among the country's best schools. But in later years, its standards declined. The school's bursar, Buba Sanneh, told us that if a student's overall average for a year was 30 or above (on a scale of 0 to 100) that student would be promoted.

Amie finished high school with seven F's and two D's on the nationwide grade twelve exam. She also had been very uncooperative with our manager, hardly ever attending the weekend tutoring classes. We didn't offer to sponsor her in any further education, and she dropped from our sight.

Years later, in April 2012, as I was buying a box of matches at a shop in Salikenni, a voice behind me called out my name. I turned, and it was Amie. She recently had been hired by the nursery school in the village, operated by a group from Germany, to work in their computer lab. The German group had provided 12 desktop computers and a wireless Internet connection. The computer room was being used as an Internet café, where anyone in the village could buy time. Amie had been hired to maintain the computers and show people how to use them.

Late one evening, Fatou Janneh, Fatou Darboe and I visited Amie in her family compound. She was quieter than I had remembered, still confident but not bubbling with her earlier enthusiasm. She told us that after high school she had taken a three-month basic course and then a six-month course in computers at Humanities First, a private college in the metropolitan area. She said these were paid for by Ebrima Ceesay, an uncle who lived abroad.

"Now I can operate a computer," she said. "I can even teach someone who does not know how, to operate a computer."

I asked her what went wrong in high school.

"Nothing went wrong," she said. "I tried my level best. I studied day and night. I studied at the National Library." She said she didn't attend the SSF weekend classes because she had her own "study teacher."

Fatou Janneh repeated the same questioning in Mandinka, hoping to draw out more information. She got essentially the same answers. We still don't know the reason for Amie's failure in high school.

During the first few years of SSF we didn't have an explicit policy on the education of girls. Our first manager, Momodou Kalleh, tended to select more boys than girls, possibly because parents sought his assistance mostly for their boys. As of March 1998, we had 24 boys in the program and 13 girls.

I had read academic studies on the benefits of girls' education to a society and to the alleviation of poverty. The World Bank has long argued that reducing gender discrimination in education in poor countries boosts economic development and results in healthier children, who themselves are more likely to be educated.

Along the way, a few people have suggested that we convert SSF into a program exclusively for girls, arguing that, with this as the goal, we would be able to raise much more in donations. But that would not have met the needs of people in the village, where both boys and girls frequently drop out of school for financial reasons. So the policy that Alison and I evolved was to provide equal opportunity for boys and girls in the program.

After Fatou Janneh became manager in 2005 we applied this policy more rigorously. Every year since then Alison and I have decided how many students to admit in grade seven based on our budget, and we have sent instructions that the student intake be equally divided between boys and girls.

But we soon found that, with some individual exceptions, our scholarship girls were having much more difficulty in their education than were the boys. Their performance in school was generally poorer. In 2009 all seven of our girls who took the grade nine exam failed. In 2010 all eight of our girls failed. In 2011 two of our girls took the exam and both failed.

More recently the girls have done much better. In each of the years 2012 and 2013, five SSF girls took the grade nine exam and in both years they all passed. Their average scores were not as good as those achieved by the boys. Still, this was a big improvement. We attribute it to several factors: The Salikenni school, under its principal, Sainey Fatajo, seems to be gradually improving. Librarian Fatou Darboe has been working with SSF girls in the village to improve their reading ability. Tutoring visits to Salikenni by some of our senior students have become established, and more boys and girls attend these sessions. Finally, everyone connected with SSF who visited the village in recent years, including Fatou Janneh, the new management team and visitors from America, has made a special effort to meet with the girls and encourage them.

We know that inability to read is a big factor in the relatively poor performance of girls. And SSF clearly needs to devote more resources to remedial reading in the future. But why are so many more girls than boys coming out of grade six in Salikenni almost unable to read?

Over the years we have asked a great many people—students, parents, educators, Gambians and experts abroad—about the education problems of girls in our program. We have received the same answers over and over again:

- Girls are given too much domestic work. When a Salikenni boy goes home at the end of a school day he has a choice: He can play football or study. A girl may have to help with the cooking, pound grain, fetch water, or wash and iron clothes for the compound.

- Some people in the village tell us there is still an old belief that education is not so important for girls "because they can always get married." Yet many parents say they counsel their daughters not to marry until they finish their education. And they tell us they will not give their daughters too much household work.

In SSF we have had several cases of girls becoming pregnant. We have always offered to let the girl continue her education. But usually the pregnancy brings education to an end. One girl whom we took into the program in grade eight in Salikenni became pregnant the following year. She did not take the grade nine exam that year. It was rumored that the baby's father was a teacher who had since left the school. He reportedly offered to marry her, but the girl's father did not agree to the marriage. She delivered a baby girl, who eventually was placed in the care of our student's grandmother. The student repeated grade nine in Salikenni, at our expense. We noted that she was a very poor reader. She failed the exam at the end of grade nine, and that ended her education.

Some have suggested to us that the Muslim religion makes girls reluctant to compete with boys in school. But when Ousman Jarju, our current manager, and I asked Salikenni's deputy imam if Islam teaches girls not to compete in school, he said, "Absolutely not. They can compete equally."

Alison and I have gradually come to the view that the problem is fundamentally one of expectations—among parents, teachers and the girls themselves. Probably starting in the early primary grades, expectations for girls are lower than they are for boys. I once asked a male teacher at the Salikenni school why so many girls were struggling in their education. He shrugged and said, "Well, they are girls."

Even among our male students there is a certain amount of ambivalence towards girls' education. I remember an occasion when Fatou Janneh led a mostly male group of our students in a discussion about the importance of education. With a little coaxing she drew from the students many answers—jobs, future income, informed voting in a democracy, awareness of other lands and cultures, and national economic development. She then turned the discussion to studies showing the economic development value of educating women. When the group seemed to accept that, Fatou asked with a smile: "Would you marry a woman who had more education than you?" There was dead silence. Then Ebrima M. Fatty, our agricultural student, said in a loud voice: "No!" The entire room erupted in laughter.

When we ask our highly successful girls why so many other girls fail, they say it is a matter of determination.

Jainaba Dibba, one of the original group of SSF students, now a graduate of Gambia College and a full-time teacher, says it is true that girls are given more domestic work than boys. But she adds, "I did all that. I went to the rice fields daily and to the vegetable garden. I had the determination. Ever since primary school, I had the goal to go into higher education. I think some of the girls today do not have the determination to go to school or to read."

Jainaba has been part of a guidance and counseling group at her school. In that role she has frequently talked with girls and encouraged them to set high goals for their own education. "I use myself as a role model," she says.

———— ✦✦✦ ————

The Gambian government has taken a series of steps to encourage the education of girls. Since 2004 it has given free tuition to girls in rural schools and some suburban parts of the country. SSF does not have to pay for its girls at the Salikenni school. We bring them into the program anyway, to maintain equality, and to begin working with them, because they will need our assistance to attend any of the Kombos high schools.

Fatoumata Fatty, whom SSF sponsored from grade seven through her first year at the university, at which point she was awarded a government scholarship to complete her undergraduate degree, commented, "Girls now have more opportunity than boys. So let them use their opportunity."

Mariama Ceesay, whom we sponsored in medical school until she received a government scholarship, believes the amount of domestic work required of girls in many families remains a problem. "Their parents are not aware of the importance of education," she said. "The only time they have for education is during school hours. After school they only do domestic work."

Some of the girls in our program do have high expectations for themselves, and they pursue their goals despite setbacks.

Sarjo Fatajo is a poised young woman with a warm smile. She attended Arabic classes in Salikenni for two years before starting grade one at the government school. For several years she attended both school systems—English school in the morning, Arabic in the afternoon. She can speak, read and write Arabic. She joined SSF in grade eight. She was obviously very bright, but she got a disappointing 46 on the WAEC exam in 2009. When the following school year began, she did not contact Fatou Janneh. We thought she might have dropped out. But that February she turned up on Fatou's doorstep and asked if she still was in the program. It turned out she was repeating grade nine at a Kombos school, at her father's expense. Fatou welcomed Sarjo to SSF's weekend classes. She attended these regularly. At the end of that year she got a 40 on the exam—not great, but it got her into Muslim Senior Secondary School, and Fatou Janneh restored her scholarship. Sarjo set her heart on studying economics and business at the university. She finished high school in 2012, with results not quite good enough for the university.

The following year, under our sponsorship, Sarjo took access courses at a private school to improve her English and math skills. These results again fell short of the university's requirements. Sarjo then wanted to enroll in a very demanding accounting course at a local business college. The student-led SSF board declined to sponsor this, feeling she was not up to it. Sarjo later applied to enter Gambia College's free program that trains secondary school teachers. SSF has offered to give her any extra help she might need in this three-year program. She has promised to return often to the SSF campus to encourage younger girls. We believe she will become a great teacher.

Aja Touray, a very slender girl, scored 43 on the WAEC exam in Salikenni, missing the cutoff by one point. She and her family, on their own initiative, decided that Aja should repeat a grade in a Kombos school. But she was not content to repeat just grade nine. She proposed that she repeat both grades eight and nine, to make sure she would be well prepared for high school. We agreed to pay for this undertaking, which took considerable courage and maturity on her part. At a meeting of SSF Kombos students, Fatou Janneh said Aja had taken a "bold step," and Aja received a round of loud applause. She has attended the Kombos classes regularly. In the fall of 2013 she again took the grade nine exam, and this time she got a 26, well within the pass mark on the backwards scale. As this is written, she has just started high school. When I phoned to congratulate her, she said her goal is to attend the university and become a television journalist.

CHAPTER 8

Jobs

THE FOLLOWING CONVERSATION is one I have had dozens, perhaps hundreds, of times in The Gambia. I meet a young man, maybe while riding in a commercial van or on a ferryboat or on a street anywhere in the country. We chat briefly, and then I ask about his education.

"I finished high school three years ago," the young man says.

"That's wonderful! What are you doing now?"

"Nothing."

The Gambia has a huge number of young men and women with some education who are doing "nothing."

According to a World Bank study (*Youth Employment and Skills Development in The Gambia, 2011*) the jobless rate in 2008 among Gambians between the ages of 15 and 24 who were not in school was 31 percent. In the urban area it was 36 percent. Few of these young people were technically unemployed. That term, in The Gambia as in the United States, includes only those actively seeking work. The technical youth unemployment rate in The Gambia in 2008 was only 3 percent. The bank reached its jobless figure by adding 33 percent of the age group whom it called "inactive," that is, those who were simply doing nothing.

For a narrower age group, 20 to 24, the bank's jobless rate of those not in school was 43 percent nationally, 50 percent in the urban area. That is a huge fact of life in The Gambia, a country in which 60 percent of the population is under the age of 25.

Yet these figures do not really tell the whole story. Nearly 70 percent of Gambian youths between the ages of 15 and 24 who are counted as employed work in agriculture. Almost all of them are subsistence farmers and thus are vastly underemployed.

One does not need statistics to see The Gambia's jobless problem—just look at the groups of young men on city street corners chatting in the middle of the day.

—◆◆◆◆—

Another experience I often have had: I walk down a crowded street in Banjul. A young man approaches with a half dozen belts draped over one arm.

"Good price," he says.

"Sorry, I have a belt."

The young man moves on. He probably comes from a village much like Salikenni and came to the big city hoping for something more lucrative than farming. I watch him make his way down the street. I don't see anyone buying his belts. I doubt that he will sell very many of them.

On another street a young woman approaches, selling cold drinking water in small plastic bags. I don't know where the water comes from, and I don't buy any.

The young man and woman are part of The Gambia's so-called informal economy, in which few records are kept, cash is the medium, and prices are negotiable. The informal sector includes rural farmers and urban petty traders and many laborers. In 2008–09 it represented 87 percent of employment in the country. As noted in the Gambia Education Country Status Report, by the World Bank, UNESCO and the Gambian Ministry of Basic and Secondary Education in 2011 (page 60), only 13 percent of jobs were in the formal sector—government, banks and large businesses.

When our students have finished their education, whether from high school or beyond, it has been to this small formal sector that they have applied for jobs. Currently, the sector isn't nearly big enough to accommodate all the students coming out of high school, business colleges and the university.

In Chapter 2 I described the difficulties that Amadou Njie, our first graduate from the university, has had finding a job in economic policy, the field in which he is trained, and his decision to take what he regards as a temporary high school teaching job. Essa Samateh, who grew up in the same compound in Salikenni as Amadou and shared the same one-room "house" with him while both were in high school, has had an even harder time.

Essa was a good-natured, polite young man, but his high school record fell short of the university's admission requirements. We sponsored him instead in a series of six-month business college courses. He earned a certificate and diplomas in three levels of commercial courses. The school offered two more levels, but we felt it was time for Essa to look for a job.

I did not see Essa again for nearly two years. In April 2012 he came to a guest house in Sukuta, where I was renting a room. He told me he had been unable to find a job. Even before he had finished his last course, he had submitted an application to a large commercial bank in Banjul. He had an interview there. The interviewer, a man, told him he would be called in later for an exam. That call never came. After several weeks he went back to the bank and was told that the interviewer had left the country, a woman now was in charge of hiring, and there were no job vacancies. Essa was convinced the new recruiter was hiring only women.

Essa then went to an uncle, Lamin Dibba, who works for a nongovernmental organization that deals with women's issues, and asked him for help finding a job. Dibba said he had a friend at the Personnel Management Office, the government's central hiring agency. Essa filed an application. The office said, "We'll call you." But, again, a call never came.

At that time Essa was living in New Yundun, in the metropolitan suburbs, in the family compound of another uncle, Bubacarr Ceesay, who was living in Italy. The family was giving Essa food and lodging, but he had no income. He had a friend who owned a clothing shop in Serrekunda. He went there almost every day, finding small ways to help out, but he received no salary. Once in a while the owner would give him a few dalasis to cover his fare.

"I'm not comfortable at all," Essa told me. "I should have a job. I feel very uncomfortable with this situation."

I advised him—based on my own experience looking for my first job—to apply for work in many more places, to go to all the banks plus other businesses and all the government agencies he could think of. He said he would.

I saw him a year later, in April 2013. "I'm managing," he said. He still had not found a permanent job. He had taken my advice and applied to more places—the Gambia Revenue Authority, the Gambia Civil Aviation Network, a generator and air conditioning company, and most recently, a company licensed by the government to buy groundnuts from farmers.

He had found a temporary job as a poll worker during the 2012 parliamentary elections and subsequent local elections. He applied for temporary work in The Gambia's ten-year census, then starting up, but was told he had not filed early enough.

"I'm discouraged," Essa said. But he kept searching, and in the summer of 2013 his luck began to improve. He landed a six-month contract job, helping to conduct a survey of 54 health facilities in The Gambia to track changes in the number of malaria cases in recent years. When I last saw him, in November 2013, he told me he expected that this contract, under the London-based Medical Research Council, would be renewed.

Yusupha Ceesay's story is similar to Essa's, except that his higher education was in computers. Yusupha joined SSF in grade eight in Salikenni. We put him through high school in the metropolitan area. He had his heart set on the university, but his grades did not meet its admission standard. We sponsored him in a certificate-level course in computers at a local business and technical school, then in a course in computer networking, and then in one in computer systems administration. He completed the courses in 2011. But when I last saw him, a year later, he had found no permanent job. Instead, he had found a temporary job with the Gambian Electoral Commission, helping to set up a voter registration database. He also worked occasionally at an Internet café owned by a friend, but his earnings there were small.

According to the World Bank, 48 percent of Gambians were living in poverty in 2010. In the rural part of the country the poverty rate was 74 percent. In approximate terms, this means living on less than $1 a day.

Education is supposed to be a long-term cure for poverty. Salikenni students, their parents, and we as sponsors of SSF, all believe this to be true. Enrollments have been rising year after year at all levels of education in The Gambia. But the number of jobs, especially in the formal sector, has not kept pace with the number of students coming out of the schools, the colleges and the university. That is a situation that only the Gambian economy and its outside donors and investors can remedy.

The Gambian economy is a narrow one, based primarily on tourism, agriculture and the re-export of goods through the port of Banjul to other African countries. Tourism declined sharply during the global recession that began in 2008, but now seems to be recovering. Agricultural output fell 60 percent during the drought that hit this part of Africa during the 2011–12 growing season. The re-export industry faces the reality that other African countries are building up their own port and transport networks. The Gambia has virtually no natural resources, although the government has for many years held out hope of someday developing offshore oil.

A big dose of private investment from abroad would help create more jobs, but The Gambia is not in the top tier of African countries with strong climates for business investment. The International Finance Corporation, the branch of the World Bank that deals with the private sector, ranks The Gambia 147th out of 185 countries around the world in terms of "ease of doing business" (www.doingbusiness.org/data). Freedom House lists The Gambia as "not free" politically (*Freedom in the World 2013*). The U.S. Department of State's 2013 Country Report on Human Rights Practices in The Gambia cites problems including "government interference with the electoral process; government harassment and abuse of its critics; and torture, arrest, detention, and sometimes enforced disappearance of its citizens."

The Gambia has been a parliamentary democracy since its independence from Britain in 1965. But it has tended toward long-term rule. Dawada Jawara was the country's elected leader for the first 30 years, initially as prime minister, then as president. During his tenure The Gambia followed the economic prescriptions of the World Bank and International Monetary Fund, reducing its fiscal deficit and increasing foreign earnings.

In 1994 Jawara was ousted in a coup by a group of soldiers who claimed they had not been paid. They were led by Yahya Jammeh, an army lieutenant. Jawara was given refuge on a U.S. Navy ship, which happened to be in the Banjul harbor on a courtesy call.

Two years later Jammeh was elected as civilian president, and he has been in power since. He was reelected in November 2011, for a fifth five-year term. His party, the Alliance for Patriotic Reorientation and Construction, retained its majority in the National Assembly in March 2012.

Former president Jawara lived in exile in England for many years. In 2001 President Jammeh granted him amnesty and invited him to return and live in The Gambia. Jawara returned in 2002 at the age of 78 and was widely welcomed as the Father of the Nation. In

2009 he published his autobiography. President Jammeh attended the festivities for the book release and bought multiple copies.

⸺◆•••◆⸺

If you visit The Gambia's tourist areas—a series of hotels and resorts scattered along the country's short Atlantic coastline—you will see another aspect of the youth unemployment problem. Tourism is, by some measures, The Gambia's biggest foreign exchange earner and one of the major employers in the formal economy. But you will often see, hanging around the hotels and on their private beaches, young men who are not on the hotel staffs. They hustle the tourists, often offering to be their guides, hoping for small amounts of money. They are known as "beach bumsters." The hotels try to chase them off the beaches. There have been articles in Gambian newspapers deploring the young men's actions on the grounds that they scare away tourists.

One of our former scholarship students is reported by several people who know him to have become, at least temporarily, a beach bumster. He heatedly denies this, so I won't use his name. We had sponsored him at the Salikenni school, through high school in the Kombos and then in several business courses.

He apparently made a diligent search for a permanent job, including applying to the government's hiring agency. "They never called me back," he told me when I saw him on one of my recent visits. He applied to all the major hotels. Only one gave him an interview, and nothing came of it. He was living with a relative in the metropolitan area, who gave him free food and lodging. To earn a bit of money, he said, "I do my own business with people." He was very reluctant to describe this business, except to say that a couple of times people had paid him to fill out application forms for them. When I asked if he had hustled tourists at the beaches he replied angrily: "Who told you that? I never do that. I never go there."

CHAPTER 9

Coming to the Kombos

WHEN OUR SCHOLARSHIP STUDENTS finish grade nine and come to the Kombos, the urban area, for high school, they face challenges that are difficult for outsiders to imagine. The challenges involve academics, culture, language, and sometimes just getting enough to eat.

Usually these students live in the Kombos with members of their extended families. Most of these relatives are poor. Some are petty traders. They are often overwhelmed by requests to send money back to Salikenni and to provide housing for students and others from the village. Some depend on renting out a room to supplement their own income. And so they often cram four or five boys into one remaining room in their compounds.

The hours when meals are served sometimes do not fit the schedules of students. It is traditional for the relatives to give the students fare to go to and from school each day. But sometimes they have no money. We have seen a few cases of students who had to skip school some days for lack of fare. Some of the relatives welcome students into a supportive family atmosphere. Others ignore them and provide no adult guidance.

Some of our students are able to cope with these conditions. Amadou Njie and Ousman Jarju are examples. Others are dragged down by these problems, and their education suffers or comes to an end.

Haruna Jallow is a case in point. He is an intense young man with broad cheekbones and steady eyes. He is the same boy, mentioned in Chapter 5, who took over a grade nine class in Salikenni when there was no teacher present. He was not in our program then. The following year, 2009, he was one of three students admitted to SSF at the grade ten level. All three had passed the grade nine exam, but their families could not pay for high school.

Haruna comes from Kerr Samba Nyado, a tiny village of mud houses with thatched roofs, more than an hour's walk from Salikenni. I have not been there, but Haruna says it has only 16 compounds, and most of its residents are Fulas, like his own family. His father, Abdoulie Jallow, is a farmer and a blacksmith. Unlike most Fulas, Abdoulie does not raise cattle. He has two wives who both live in the village.

"On my mother's side we are six," Haruna told me in 2009. "The other wife has only one child." Haruna is the oldest boy. Their father was able to put one of Haruna's younger brothers, Saidou, through high school. Saidou had not been able to find a job and was "doing nothing."

The next boy down the line, Adama, had to stop school in seventh grade for lack of money and was apprenticed to an electrician. Two younger sisters, ages 12 and 8, had never been to school. Another sister was a toddler.

When Haruna was about 5, his father took him to live in the metropolitan area and put him into an Arabic school for several years. In 2001 the family moved back to Kerr Samba Nyado, which has only a nursery school. Haruna walked five kilometers every day to Minta Kunda to attend primary school. When he was ready for middle school, Momodou Kalleh, the manager of our program at that point, took Haruna into his family compound in Salikenni so that he could attend grades seven through nine there.

Haruna got a bare pass on the ninth-grade exam, but it was enough to gain him admission to Masroor Senior Secondary School, a big, relatively new high school in the far suburbs of the metropolitan area. Haruna's father, Abdoulie, had recently bought a compound in Sinchu Alhagie, within easy walking distance of the school. Abdoulie had intended to live in the new compound himself but Abdoulie's own father died. Now head of the family, Abdoulie decided to stay in Kerr Samba Nyado.

So, as he started high school, Haruna moved into his father's empty compound. Initially, his two younger brothers, Saidou and Adama, moved in as well. The three were alone in the compound. When I visited the boys that year I was repelled by the physical condition of the place. The walls of some of the buildings were crumbling. Only one house seemed habitable. It contained a couple of sagging beds and little else. The wind, laden with dust, blew right through the house. Their father had arranged with a woman in the neighborhood to cook for them, but she did not come every day.

"Sometimes we have food to eat," Haruna told me that first year. "Sometimes we don't. We talk to our parents only by [mobile] phone. My father visits once a year. If you see him two times you know it's an emergency." The boys found occasional jobs with building contractors to earn a little money for food. They never found steady work.

Haruna's first year at Masroor was an academic disaster. In the first term he got nine F's. In the second term he did slightly better, and in the third term slightly better still. But he ended the year with an average of 33.5 and was not promoted.

Haruna told us that his difficulties that first year in the Kombos were partly a matter of language. He said he and other students fresh from the provinces had trouble understanding the English spoken by the Masroor teachers. And they found it hard to express themselves in English. "It is difficult to write the answers," he said. "We know exactly what he's talking about, but it is difficult to find the words to answer. You know, sometimes you know something but you only know it in the local language." Haruna had other complaints that seemed less genuine. He said his teachers graded papers unfairly. Fatou Janneh and I told him separately that we didn't accept such excuses.

At that time, Fatou and I felt that in the recent past we had been too lax in applying our standards for academic performance, carrying too many students who were unlikely to make it. So we declined to pay for Haruna to repeat grade ten, but we told him that if his father could pay for it, and if Haruna did well, we would take him back into the program. His father did pay for the first term that year, but at midyear I learned that the remaining tuition had not been paid. Haruna's first term grades, meanwhile, were stronger than the previous year's. He got a bare pass or better in every course. On the strength of that we paid the remainder of his fee. By the end of the year he had improved further, and we officially brought him back into the program.

During the summer of 2011, while Haruna was taking classes at Masroor to prepare for grade eleven, Modou Lamin Darboe, one of our university students and a leading member of the management team, went to Masroor on his own initiative and met with Haruna. He reported that Haruna was living alone in the compound at that point. The provision of meals was still very irregular. Haruna was attending school for two days then skipping the third day in order to work as a laborer so that he would be able to afford food. Fatou Janneh and I agreed to give him a regular food allowance.

Haruna attended Fatou Janneh's weekend classes in Sukuta as often as possible. Her Saturday classes were difficult for him to attend because Masroor follows a Muslim calendar, with Friday off but with school in session on Saturday. Haruna's classes were in the afternoon session on Saturdays but he made an arrangement with a teacher at Masroor allowing him to attend school in the mornings instead. Then he walked to Sukuta, which took him at least two hours each way.

Haruna told me that he and other SSF students were receiving a lot of encouragement from our manager. "Fatou Janneh advises us as though we were her children," he said. "She is like a parent— even more than some parents. She always wants to know about our school. She always advises us to do good things and study our books. She is like a mother."

I visited the Jallow compound in Sinchu Alhagie again in April 2012. Haruna, then in grade eleven, was living there only with Adama, his younger brother. No one else lived in the compound, and I was struck again by a sense of desolation. Haruna was using the allowance Fatou Janneh gave him to buy a bag of rice at the end of each month. A woman in the next compound was cooking it, and a small boy was supposed to deliver two meals a day, lunch and dinner. But recently only one meal a day had been arriving. The bags of rice were lasting almost but not quite 31 days. There was only one serviceable bed in the compound, and the boys shared it. There was no electricity. To study at night, Haruna went to a room at the school that was kept open and lit for that purpose. Adama told me he was working in an auto repair shop, learning automotive electronics. He said he received no regular pay and no lunch. But sometimes someone would hire him for a small job and pay him maybe 100 dalasis (about 3 U.S. dollars).

Haruna said his father had visited about three months earlier and expressed worry that he was only getting one meal a day. "How can you learn?" his father asked, and urged him to give up school. "I told him I'll manage," Haruna said. "I'll manage, Inshallah by the grace of God." He said he would never give up school. "I want to be somebody," he told me. "I want to be a lawyer."

Haruna finished high school in 2013. He wanted to enroll in Gambia College's free teacher-training program. The college said his final results in grade twelve were not good enough. It recommended he repeat grade twelve and apply again the following year. Haruna agreed to follow that advice, and SSF agreed to pay for the repeat.

———— ⋅•⋅•⋅• ————

Malick Ceesay joined our program in 2002–03 in grade eight in Salikenni. He was a tall boy with deep-set eyes and only one arm. His left arm had been amputated at the shoulder when he was a young child, after an accident involving a donkey cart. His father, Dunbung Ceesay, a Salikenni farmer, said Malick would not be able to earn a living by physical work—it would have to be through education. I know of no SSF student who has had a more difficult time trying to get an education.

In the middle of his first year in SSF there was a brief student riot at the Salikenni school in which school property was damaged and a teacher was injured. Fifteen students were expelled over the incident, including Malick, although he insisted he had not taken part in it. He was out of school for the rest of that year. In 2004–05 we enrolled him in the Crab Island middle school in Banjul, where he repeated grade eight. At the end of grade nine there, he got a WAEC exam score that was just on the borderline for admission to high school. In grades ten and eleven at Gambia Senior Secondary School in Banjul he failed many of his courses.

When he was in grade eleven, I asked Malick to show me where he lived. He took me to the Tobacco Road neighborhood of Banjul. He led me to a dusty compound and into a dark room barely large enough for one bed and a short couch. Five boys shared the room. Malick was the only one who was a student. He slept on a foam mat on the floor. The only place he could find to study was the National Library, which was next door to his school. He was in the school's afternoon shift, so the logical time to go to the library was in the morning. But his compound did not serve breakfast. This is not uncommon in poor households in Banjul. The women of the compound served lunch at 2 p.m., just when Malick had to be at school. There was no food for him until he returned home after 6 p.m. Malick was spending a lot of time every morning visiting compounds where he knew someone, hoping he would be invited to share breakfast. I asked a woman who seemed to have some authority in the compound if she could somehow find a way to give Malick breakfast. She said she would, but apparently she did not.

As Malick was starting grade twelve we received word that there had been some kind of fight in the compound, and Malick had been injured. I went there and found him with a bandage pasted across one eyebrow. He had been to a nearby medical clinic. At that point, Fatou Janneh invited Malick to live in her compound. He moved into the room in the shed outside her house, furnished with a bed, a table, a chair and an electric light bulb in the ceiling. Fatou gave Malick three meals a day, laundry service and fare to go and come from school.

But by then Malick was far behind in school, and he never caught up. His grade twelve year was a failure. He asked us to enroll him in a multi-year course in business management at a local college, but Fatou and I agreed this was not a justifiable use of scholarship funds. The last I heard of Malick, he was back in Salikenni, living in his family's compound.

◆◆◆

Fatou Janneh repeatedly expressed her concern about the living conditions of our Kombos students and the impact these conditions often had on their education. In an article for the 2006 SSF annual report, she wrote:

> My own view regarding the way forward is to build a campus to serve as a residence for the students in the Kombos. This will ease the problem of housing. Such a place will also ease for the girls some of the chores that hamper their progress. They will be monitored and counseled against bad boys and men.

The campus should have an Internet café preferably for commercial and private use . . . There should be within the campus a small library . . . An adult monitor would be needed . . . This, if established, will be a model academic centre.

During the next few years, Alison and I discussed the idea of a residence for SSF students many times with Fatou and with some of our U.S. donors. Each time, we concluded that the cost of building, equipping, staffing, and providing food for such a campus was, at the time, far beyond our financial ability. Then, one day in January 2010, we received an email from Fatou:

I'm pleased to inform you that since last year I applied for a loan of 60,000 dalasis [then about $2,400] from my bank, which is just approved recently . . . As soon as I get the money, I intend to start a small housing project. It may take years, but when finished, the problem of housing for our students will be a thing of the past.

A year later, when I visited her compound, there, next to her house, stood the bare, cement-block walls of a large, unfinished building. There was no roof. The interior floors were dirt and construction rubble. Fatou showed me the layout. Interior walls had been roughed in, forming nine rooms. Some of these would house students, perhaps two to a room. There would also be a common room, a computer room, a guest room for SSF visitors, and several interior bathrooms. Fatou envisioned it as a comfortable, supervised place, conducive to learning, for a dozen or more students, both boys and girls. She would try to have a mix of some very good students and some weaker ones, who could be expected to improve in such an environment. She might include one or two of our university students, who could help supervise, chaperone, tutor, and who could also be role models.

At the end of my visit I asked Fatou to get estimates from some local builders of the cost of finishing the building. One of these put the cost at $15,000, which was more than the entire cost of our scholarship program the previous year. We thought of applying to some other organization for a grant. But there was a legal problem: The building was inside Fatou's compound. She, not SSF, would own it. We felt we could not ask donors to invest in a building that SSF would not own.

When Fatou left for England in 2013 the masonry hulk still stood unfinished in her compound.

But when the board of senior students was established, they refused to give up on the idea of somehow providing a decent place in which our high school students could live and study. At one of the board's early meetings Ousman said that the "biggest, biggest" problem SSF faced was student housing in the Kombos. "As long as accommodation remains a problem," he added, "it will be very hard for some people to make it."

At one point the senior students planned to try to raise the money for a campus themselves. They decided they would start with a fund-raising concert, featuring a local musician. They would seek donations from Gambian businessmen, the U.S. Embassy, and from Gambians living in the United States and Europe. They would ask the Salikenni parents of SSF students to create a cooperative farm on which, through joint labor, they would grow crops to be used either to sell for cash or to provide food for a campus. The students hoped to first raise enough money to buy some land in the Kombos and later enough to build the campus. "We will do it," Ousman declared. Everyone involved could see that this would take a long time.

Alison and I continued to think of the campus as something in the far future. The senior students wanted quicker action. "If we can't have a campus now," they reasoned, "what about a partial campus?"

Once they started working on this idea events moved quickly. In August 2013 Ousman learned of a compound in Serrekunda, whose owner was willing to rent eight apartments to SSF on a yearly basis. Serrekunda is the biggest of the Banjul suburbs. It resounds with commerce, big and small. It is filled with what Gambians call "story buildings"—meaning they are more than one story tall. Its market area extends for block after block. Its residential streets seem endless. The compound Ousman found is owned by Salifou Dahaba, the father of Ousman's wife, Ndey. Salifou does not live there but was renting out rooms to people who often were unable to pay him. He supports SSF's goals and was willing to offer a quite reasonable price in return for having stable tenants.

Alison and I calculated that the first year's cost of the project, including a rather spartan budget for renovation and furnishing, could indeed be afforded within the funds we expected to have available for the 2013–14 academic year; so we gave our approval. The senior students moved quickly. The campus, as all our students call it, opened for occupancy on October 1, 2013. I lived there for five days during a visit to Salikenni and the Kombos the following month.

The entrance is an iron gate on an unpaved residential street. The compound is a long, narrow rectangle. On the right-hand side is a single, long, cement-block building with a veranda running its entire length, covered by an overhanging roof. Along the veranda there are about a dozen wooden doors, each opening into a separate apartment. Each apartment has a front room, a back room, and a walled, open-air space at the rear for bathing. The left-hand side of the compound is a dirt courtyard with a small shed used for storage and cooking.

The entire building has been freshly painted, green and white outside, and a pleasing light green inside. The interior floors are covered in blue linoleum with a white design. The apartments are clean but without luxury. Each has two queen-size mattresses on the floor, a bucket for drinking water, another bucket for bathing, and not much else. The student board has stuck to a lean start-up budget for the project.

Ousman and Ndey and their daughter, Sarata, moved permanently into one apartment near the entrance to the compound. Two members of the board, Mustapha Darboe and Amadou Njie, also moved into the compound to provide further supervision, tutoring and mentoring for the high school students.

The board drew up strict rules for the compound, including: five hours a day minimum time for study, visitors only on Sundays, limited use of mobile phones, only English to be spoken on the premises, smoking prohibited, proper clothing required.

At the time of my visit, 16 SSF high school students were living in the campus, including six girls who shared two apartments near the front of the compound, under Ndey's watchful eye. In the cases of all 16 residents, Ousman and his team went to Salikenni and obtained the consent of parents. Most of the parents were enthusiastic about the campus. In choosing residents, Ousman

The recently opened SSF campus and some of its residents.

gave priority to grade ten students, newly arrived in the Kombos. He also included a few students in higher grades of high school who did very poorly last year. We hope the campus environment will help them improve.

When I asked the high school students how they liked living in the campus, each one gave the same response, a broad smile and wholehearted approval. "It's very fine," said Amadou G. Bah, whose school is a 20-minute walk away. "Here you have time to study. Ousman and Amadou and Wuyeh [Wuyeh Keita, in grade twelve] they assist us." Isatou Dibba, a girl in grade ten, said, "I'm so glad to be in this compound. I have more time to study, and I have access to laptops."

In one of the apartments the senior students arranged to have the wall between the two rooms removed, making one big space. This is the library, study and meeting room. It is equipped with two long tables placed end to end. Five SSF laptop computers, with wireless Internet connection, are available for the students to use there. The library is also used for tutoring classes on weekends.

I had time to observe the campus rhythm. Weekday mornings the students emerged from their rooms in their crisp, clean uniforms. They went to the small cookhouse beside the main building and grabbed breakfast—a long loaf of bread with good things inside and a cup of tea. Then they were off to school. At 9 p.m., after dinner in the compound, compulsory study time began in the library. One evening, as I passed by, students sat around the long tables, reading silently. The power was off. A half-dozen candles were burning on the tables, barely illuminating the faces of the students, who were deep in concentration.

On weekend mornings the students had time to do their laundry and sweep up. In the afternoon an outside teacher came in and held a class—math on Saturdays and English on Sundays.

We have to give credit for the campus entirely to the board of SSF senior students. Without their initiative we would probably still be talking about it as something in the future. The campus is a work in progress. So far it is housing only some of our high school students. Some felt their existing housing was adequate and sometimes closer to their schools. Ousman is saving space for some of next year's new grade ten students to move in. As this is written the campus needs many more books in its library and more furniture in the student rooms. What the team has built so far is at least a very good start.

The campus promises for the first time to provide our students coming to the Kombos with a decent place in which to live, the companionship of peers, an atmosphere conducive to study, and supervision, guidance and encouragement by senior students.

Ousman and I have also discussed the possibility that during summer and other holiday periods, when Kombos students often go back to Salikenni, we could bring some of our Salikenni students to the Serrekunda compound and give them intensive remedial reading help and other tutoring.

CHAPTER 10

Looking to the Future

THE STRENGTH OF SSF lies in its students, many of whom have risen to management positions. Younger students are on their way up, and many of them may eventually assume leadership roles. Following are brief portraits of just a few of these rising students who someday might become members of the board.

Kasamanding Kanteh

Kasamanding is one of our newest scholarship students. She joined SSF in November 2013, one of six girls and six boys, all in grade seven at the Salikenni school, who were admitted in our annual intake of students.

Forty-seven applicants, more than in any year before, applied for the twelve openings, indicating a growing desire for education in Salikenni and nearby villages. Members of SSF's board of senior students went to Salikenni and tested each applicant in math, English language, and reading ability. Parents and guardians were interviewed to determine each family's financial circumstances. The board selected the students. I took part in one set of interviews and am confident that the board, in every case, chose students who were in real financial need and who also had demonstrated academic ability.

Kasamanding, then approaching her 16th birthday, got the highest composite score among girls on the admission tests and the second highest among girls and boys combined. She is articulate and self-confident. She wants to be a nurse like her friend, Isatou, who works at the local health clinic. Kasamanding likes to read and often visits the SSF library in Salikenni. Her domestic chores include pounding grain and sometimes cooking for the whole family.

Her father is no longer living. Her mother, Mansalley Touray, is responsible for the compound, with six people under her care. The family grows only rice, and only enough of it for home consumption. In a good year the rice may last through the dry season, but sometimes it lasts only four or five months. Then her mother must ask neighbors for help. There is no one in the extended family on whom the family can call for assistance.

Mansalley never went to school. Five of Kassamanding's older siblings, four brothers and a sister, attended primary school, but went no farther because of lack of money. But Mansalley says education is important, and she strongly supports her daughter's goal to be educated.

Sulayman Bah

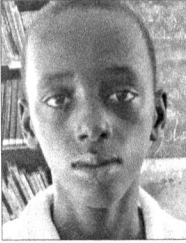

Sulayman, 14, got the best score among all applicants in the November 2013 intake of students starting grade seven at the Salikenni school. He now moves to grade eight. He comes from Dobo, an hour's walk away. Sulayman wants to be a teacher, like Mr. Njie, a Dobo primary teacher who inspired him in this goal. Specifically he would like to teach math, and social and environmental studies, his favorite subjects. He loves to play soccer on the dusty field outside the school, with nothing but wooden sticks for goals. He likes to take part in class library periods, but he has never gone to the library by himself and has never borrowed a book.

His mother, Malla Bah, said the family depends entirely on farming for a living, growing coos and groundnuts, mostly for home consumption.

Four of her children are now in school, including Sulayman, The others are in lower grades. No one in the extended family is able to help with education costs. Malla said she wants them all to be educated "to help the family out of a difficult financial situation."

Mariama Manneh

Mariama joined our program in 2012 in grade seven in Salikenni. In that year she told Mary Ann Roberts that her goal was to become "a powerful teacher." Her results in grades seven and eight have been good. Now she is starting grade nine.

Ousman recently reported: "She studies in her grandmother's room after everyone is asleep. She has created for herself a written timetable for studying each subject. She can read very well and is very punctual in study classes. She has all the time she needs for her education, not too much domestic work. During the summer she has been helping her mum in her rice field. But she has been able to create some time for books. She is very much aware of the challenges that await her in grade eight, and she is confident she will break any obstacle that might come her way. She does her studies on the floor, which is not comfortable."

Mariama's grandmother, Mai Ceesay, once told me she wanted Mariama to go to the university so she "can have a good life and take care of herself and her family." Mai Ceesay said that when school was in session, she never allowed Mariama to go with her to the rice fields but insisted she stay home and study. "I am an old woman," Mai said, "but I am strong. I don't need help."

The family is very devout. A sister, Fatumata, graduated from an Arabic language high school and now teaches in such a school. A brother, Lamin, also graduated from an Arabic high school and hopes to go on to higher Islamic studies. Mariama herself attends Arabic classes after the regular school day.

Fatou Colley

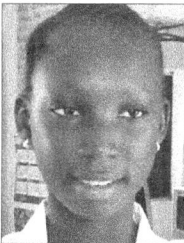

Fatou also came into SSF in 2013 in grade seven in Salikenni and now is starting grade nine there. Mary Ann Roberts wrote in her 2012 report: "Neither parent reads. Her father owns a small shop in Salikenni, selling staples such as sugar. What she enjoys most is learning.

Her favorite subjects are science and English. Fatou is unsure what she wants to be. No one ever asked her that before. We went to her compound and met her father, who was very appreciative of the scholarship. Fatou came to our compound to wish us safe travel home." From Ousman: "Fatou is well prepared for the challenges of grade eight and promises to work extra hard." Fatou told me that two of her older brothers, Ebrima and Basiru, both dropped out before finishing high school. Awa, a sister, did finish high school and then met a man who took her to Libya. She now lives with him there.

Aminata Njie

Many of our students set their career goals very high. Aminata is a talented student, now starting grade nine in Salikenni. Back when she was in grade seven, she told me in a confident voice that her goal was to become a secretary general. Had she heard of the United Nations? Yes, but she didn't want to try to describe it. I told her that she could, indeed, become anything she wanted. We discussed women who are doctors and judges and presidents of countries, including The Gambia's current vice-president, who is a woman. Aminata smiles easily and speaks clearly. Her grade seven and eight results have been good. She studies every night at home and regularly attends SSF's after-school tutoring classes. Her father, Fafanding Njie, was educated only as far as third grade. Somehow he learned a fair amount of English. He told me in English that Aminata could become "a doctor or anything, a president, a vice-president." He wants her to go to the university.

Nyima Njie

Nyima, who is not directly related to Aminata, above, also is beginning grade nine in Salikenni. Nyima's parents have tried to educate all their children. But all her older siblings except one had to drop out for lack of money. Demba, Foday and Maimie stopped at grade eleven, Omie at eight, Aja at nine. The only one who did not drop out was Buba Njie, who has been under SSF scholarship since grade seven. He has just finished high school, and we are sponsoring him to study accounting at Management Development Institute, a local business college. Nyima wants to attend the university and become a nurse. She is a good student. In grade seven she was a member of the Drama Club, also interchangeably known as the Press Club. She likes being a club member. She studies at home a minimum of thirty minutes every night.

Ebrima Marong

Ebrima joined SSF in the fall of 2011, when he was in grade seven in Salikenni. He has consistently been one of our top students, generally scoring in the 80s and 90s in most subjects. As this is written, he is completing grade nine in Salikenni and is about to head off for high school. He is small in build, with alert eyes and a polite, eager manner. He comes from the village of Mandori. His parents are farmers. He is the youngest of four children and the only one of them in school. His two older brothers and older sister are working on the farm. But his parents strongly support his education. He has told me he wants to be a doctor. Mary Ann Roberts was impressed with Ebrima's enthusiasm for learning when she visited Salikenni in 2011 and engaged his class—then grade seven—in a word game with flash cards. She recalls him "eagerly leaning forward, arms waving to be called on to answer each question." She wrote in her notebook that he was "very likely to succeed given any opportunity."

On a return visit to the village in 2012, Mary Ann noted "a deeper seriousness" in Ebrima. She asked the then grade eight class to write something about themselves in journals she had given each one. "As others were struggling to put thoughts on paper," she wrote, "Ebrima wrote on and on without hesitation. As he was finishing I asked if he would share his journal writing with me, and he read aloud to me. He had written long and beautifully about who he was, what his strengths were, and how he wanted to make a difference in life. His hero was Nelson Mandela, and he knew the man and the history well and incorporated Mandela's courage and strength into his own written dream." Returning to the United States, Mary Ann bought him a copy of Mandela's autobiography, which I delivered to him the following year.

Yunusa Bah

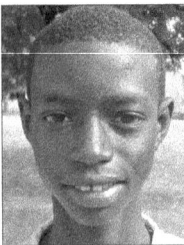

Yunusa, a slender boy from Dobo, is another of our top students, finishing grade nine in Salikenni and about to go off to high school. Already he is becoming a student leader. In April 2013, Ousman and I went to Dobo to meet ten SSF students who were living there. We also met their parents, who told us that students from Dobo found it hard or impossible to attend SSF's afternoon tutoring classes in Salikenni, because of their schedules in school and their hour's walk to and from school every day. They asked if we could hire a teacher to hold tutoring classes in Dobo. We said we could not, but we proposed an alternative—that the SSF students in Dobo join together and hold study classes among themselves, with the stronger students helping the weaker ones. The parents and students welcomed the idea.

Yunusa, on his own, quickly emerged as the organizer of these study classes. He came to me the next day in Salikenni and said the students would need books and candles to study at night, as there is no electricity in Dobo. I arranged for him to borrow a set of supplementary textbooks in each subject from the library. And we bought him a supply of candles.

Yunusa's father, Demba Bah, told me in 2011 that he had eight children, four of whom were going to school. Yunusa was the farthest along in his education.

In 2012 I noticed that Yunusa's eyes were very red, and he seemed to be having trouble focusing on a page. We took him to an eye doctor in the metropolitan area, who diagnosed the condition as vernal catarrh, in this case an over-sensitivity to ultraviolet light. The doctor prescribed a long course of medication, which we paid for and which seems to be controlling the condition.

Alieu Darboe

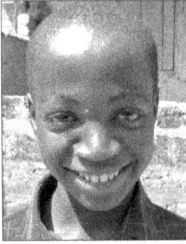

Alieu is starting grade eleven at Nusrat Senior Secondary School in the metropolitan area. He grew up in Salikenni and has been in our program since grade seven there. In 2013 he got an aggregate score of 12 on the grade nine exam in Salikenni. In the Gambian way of scoring, this is equivalent to an A average over eight subjects. He once told me that he wanted to be a doctor. But at Nusrat he has chosen a commerce course, rather than science.

Alieu is small, very outgoing and eager. His father, for many years a teacher of the Koran at the Salikenni school, taught him Arabic before he started primary school. Alieu can read and write Arabic but does not speak it. When he was a young boy, one of his first chores was to carry lunch out to his older brothers as they spent the day working on their farm.

When Mary Ann Roberts and her husband, Bill Babcock, were in Salikenni during November 2012, they proposed that the grade nine SSF students hold an election, by secret ballot, to choose the most responsible student among them. The group had never before voted in an election. Alieu won by a clear majority. His prize was Bill's old, personal championship soccer ball, for Alieu to manage and for all to enjoy.

Jainaba Faye

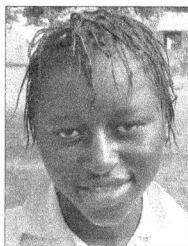

Jainaba comes from the village of Bani, which has only a primary school. She has been in our program since grade seven, attending the Salikenni school. One of her sisters lives in Salikenni, and Jainaba has stayed with her while school was in session. Jainaba has consistently been one of the best students among girls in the SSF program. Now she is finishing grade nine and is about to start high school. She wants to be a doctor.

In April 2012, Jainaba and I traveled by donkey cart from Salikenni to Bani so I could meet her family. Bani is a small village and very dusty. We stopped on a sand lane, and she ushered me into a large compound, which was pleasantly shaded by a huge mango tree.

Her mother, Fiedy Cham, is a large woman with a kind face and a firm handshake. She is a widow and presides over the compound. Fiedy wanted to educate all of her children, but that has been a struggle. One of Jainaba's sisters, Jele, dropped out in grade nine because there was no money to pay her school fee. A brother, Siaka, never went to school and now drives a jitney van between Salikenni and Bara, across the river from Banjul. Another brother, Kemba, almost made it through high school. He was in the compound the day of my visit, a pleasant, articulate young man. He told me that a "cousin brother" had been paying his fees through high school, a bit at a time. Kemba was sent out of school several times because the payments were late. Near the end of grade twelve his benefactor "had a problem." Kemba's fees went unpaid the entire year, so he could not take the exam or graduate. He gave up and worked at odd jobs for awhile, and then he, too, became first an *aprendi* and then a driver of one of the Salikenni-Bara vans.

Kemba told me his story without a trace of self-pity. He said he has high hopes for Jainaba's education and also for that of Sana and Sainey, Fiedy's twelve-year-old twin boys. Sana now goes to the English primary school in Dobo. Sainey, by his own choice, attends an Arabic school there. He wants to be an Arabic teacher.

Fiedy strongly supports Jainaba's ambition to go to the university and become a doctor, even though she knows how many years it will take before Jainaba can begin supporting the family. She said she does not want Jainaba's dream to be cut short the way Kemba's was. Again and again she expressed her gratitude for our sponsorship of Jainaba. As I left the compound she handed me a beautiful, plump, white, live chicken.

⚬⚬⚬

As I rode back to Salikenni on the donkey cart, I thought of the reverence that people in these villages have for education, and the depth of their gratitude to anyone who helps them move toward that goal. I thought of our senior students, who have been helped in their own education by SSF, and who now work to keep the program going for new generations. I thought of SSF's donors who, over many years, have made substantial progress possible. The chicken was for them, too.

As the donkey plodded along the sand road, the driver raised his stick and shouted, "*Acha!*" and the cart moved a little faster, I knew it had all been worthwhile.

The Salikenni family now included all of us—new students, senior students, donors, volunteers, administrators and advisors. I was confident in the belief that we all will continue to pull together to help meet the educational needs of these communities as they evolve.

The Salikenni Scholarship Fund is an ongoing story. To learn more about the program and see the latest information about our students, please visit our website:

www.salikenni.org

www.ingramcontent.com/pod-product-compliance
Lightning Source LLC
Chambersburg PA
CBHW031508270326
41930CB00006B/308